GOD'S BOOK OF WISDOM

To order additional copies of
God's Book of Wisdom,
by
Jonathan Oey and Kathleen Kiem Hoa Oey Kuntaraf,
call
1-800-765-6955.

Visit us at
www.reviewandherald.com
for information on other Review and Herald® products.

GOD's
BOOK
of
WISDOM

JONATHAN OEY **KUNTARAF**
KATHLEEN KIEM HOA OEY **KUNTARAF**
with LOIS MOORE

REVIEW AND HERALD® PUBLISHING ASSOCIATION
HAGERSTOWN, MD 21740

The Review and Herald Publishing Association publishes biblically based materials for
spiritual, physical, and mental growth and Christian discipleship.

The author assumes full responsibility for the accuracy of all facts and quotations as cited
in this book.

This book was
Edited by Gerald Wheeler
Copyedited by James Cavil
Cover design by Trent Truman
Cover art by Lars Justinen
Electronic makeup by Shirley M. Bolivar
Typeset: Bembo 11/13

PRINTED IN U.S.A.
11 10 09 08 07   5 4 3 2 1

R&H Cataloging Service
Kuntaraf, Jonathan Oey, 1947-   .
          God's book of wisdom
by Jonathan Oey Kuntaraf and Kathleen Kiem Hoa Oey Kuntaraf
with Lois Moore.

     1. Bible—Study and teaching.   2. Bible—Evidences,
Authority, etc.   I. Kuntaraf, Kathleen Kiem Hoa Oey, 1946-   .
II. Moore, Lois   III. Title
                    220.1

ISBN 10: 0-8280-2017-5
ISBN 13: 978-0-8280-2017-6

CONTENTS

INTRODUCTION

Trust seems to be a real problem for many people. Citizens do not trust their government leaders, members do not trust their pastors, husbands and wives do not trust each other, children do not trust their parents and vice versa—and the list goes on. Is there anything left that we can trust in today's secular society? Yes: we can trust the Bible! We can believe the Bible through personal experience.

I grew up in a Chinese Indonesian home; I lived as a Buddhist until I was 6 years old. When my parents converted to a Protestant religion, my father was baptized first; my mother and I followed later. Until I was 17 years old I fellowshipped with the Methodists, among whom I learned about grace, and the Pentecostals, from whom I learned about "the enthusiasm of having His grace." I still vividly remember rushing home from the church when I was 17, kneeling beside my bed, and praying, "Jesus, I believe in You! But what should I do next?" A few days later I found a flyer on my front doorstep advertising an evangelistic meeting to begin that very evening. I felt it was God's answer to my prayer. By the second meeting I was enthralled by what I was learning, and I continued studying until I was baptized into the Seventh-day Adventist Church in September 1964.

Thus began my journey of trust in the Bible and my joyful walk with Jesus, which still continues.

Back in 1964 Adventists were commonly known as "people of the Book." The expression originally came from the Koran, referring to the three monotheistic religions, Judaism, Christianity, and Islam. "Do not dispute with the people of the Book; . . . say, 'We believe in what has been sent down to us and what has been sent down to you; our God and your God is one' " (Sura 29.45). But in the past many applied the phrase "people of the Book" to Adventists because they studied their Bibles. Sadly, a different picture emerges today.

7

The findings of the Barna research study of June 2001 should concern us. Comparing seven religious practices of 12 major denominations, the Barna study concluded that Seventh-day Adventists ranked seventh in frequency of Bible reading, and only twelfth in prayer activities. The Barna study correlates with one coordinated by the General Conference that shows that only a small percentage of our members have a consistent devotional life. Sadly, these studies indicate that Seventh-day Adventists are no longer "people of the Book."

We need to come back to the Book—the Bible. It is estimated that our church membership will reach 50 million by the year 2020, and of that number, only 12 percent will have an Adventist heritage. Thus the majority of our members in 2020 will be first-generation Adventists. It will be vitally important to nurture them in their spiritual growth by increasing their trust in the Bible as the Word of God.

The Bible changes lives! Its teachings have totally altered life in some communities around the world. When trusted as God's Word, it has the power to energize and motivate people to live the kind of lives that will glorify God.

We live in an increasingly sophisticated and educated world. How then can we trust in the ancient writings of the Bible? Is it sufficient for us to know *what* we believe? We must explore ways to increase trust in the Bible so that we also know *why* we believe. This book was written to meet this challenge.

—Jonathan Oey Kuntaraf

CHAPTER 1

Divine Ways of Communication

God had a problem! He had created everything perfectly. The Bible expresses the beauty of His marvelous work by declaring, "God saw everything that He had made, and indeed it was very good" (Gen. 1:31, NKJV). But when sin entered our world, His face-to-face communication with His children became impossible. How, then, could He talk with those He loved? If you had been in His situation, what methods would you have chosen? Write messages in the sky? Thunder your voice? Use miracles to show your love? Talk to special people and have them write down what you told them?

As you readily recognize, God has used adaptations of all of these approaches. Elisha's servant saw the hills full of angel chariots surrounding the city (2 Kings 6:17). It was a miraculous revelation of God's caring love. Another time God thundered His voice from Mount Sinai, along with lightning and a loud trumpet blast (Ex. 19:16). His miracles appear in nearly every book of the Bible, from preserving Noah and his family in an ark to the apostles' healings and raising of the dead.

He Sent His Prophets

The Lord used prophets to improve the divine-human relationship. In fact, prophetic ministry was God's idea and initiative, as He sought to reduce the great gap between Him and His rebellious family on earth. Although He employed various methods to communicate with human beings, the prophet was the most recognized form. "Surely the Lord God does nothing, unless He reveals His secret to His servants the prophets" (Amos 3:7, NKJV).

How do we know that God worked through prophets? The Bible tells us!

But can we trust what the Bible declares? Later we will study evidences

9

for this. Let's hold that question for now and just look at *how* God has revealed Himself to prophets.

An interesting word study with a concordance reveals at least three major methods (and several variations of them) by which God presented His messages to His prophets. One involves dreams, and He used it with more than just His "official" prophets. Abimelech (Gen. 20:3-6) and Joseph (Gen. 37:5; 40:5; and 41:7, 8) are two examples. You will remember, too, the soldier who dreamed of a barley loaf smashing into the Midian camp (Judges 7:13-15), as well as newly appointed King Solomon's dream (1 Kings 3:5). God also used dreams to communicate with His regular prophets (Jer. 23:28; Dan. 7:1).

Does this mean that everyone who dreams has received personal communication from God? Hardly! But God does sometimes disclose His plans for His children through dreams.

Remember Daniel's visions of beasts, thrones, and such? Yes, God also employed visions. Strong's concordance acknowledges a vision as to mental perception, or the receiving of an "oracle" or "revelation" or "the act of seeing, having experiences, or gazing." It is likely that when prophets announced that "the word of the Lord . . . came" to them (Jer. 46:1; Hosea 1:1; Joel 1:1; Micah 1:1, etc.), it often did so in the form of a vision, as when Amos 1:1 tells us "the words of Amos . . . which he saw . . ." How could Amos see words? Did God write them out and show them to him in a vision? Not likely! Amos probably saw a heavenly being talking with him, and he heard the words. Remember that Jesus, the "Word," became flesh (John 1:14). Dreams, visions, "seeing" the Word, the Word coming to us . . . God has used all these methods to draw His children back into relationship with Him through warning, reproof, and teaching.

God Is Seeking People

The images of people looking for their loved ones or pets after the destruction of Hurricanes Katrina and Rita are still vivid in people's minds. What rejoicing when they were reunited. Even more poignant is God's seeking for us. That's His whole purpose in wanting to establish communication—so that He can find and rescue us from our terrible plight. Here is probably one of the most appealing aspects of Christianity to members of other religions. Instead of having to be appeased or placated, He *is seeking us because He loves us.* He called to Adam and Eve in the Garden of Eden, asking, "Where are you?" Listen to Jeremiah relaying God's words: "And the Lord has sent to you all His servants the prophets, . . . but you have not listened (Jer. 25:4, NKJV). Isaiah speaks for Him, crying, "Turn to me and be saved" (Isa. 45:22, RSV), and again, "Come, all who are thirsty" (Isa. 55:1, NEB). Jesus' parables show God as a merchant seeking fine pearls (Matt. 13:45, 46), as a king sending servants to invite guests to a banquet (Matt. 22:2-9), or as one seeking a lost coin or sheep (Luke 15:1-10). Revelation portrays the Spirit and the bride declaring, "Come" (Rev. 22:17). Yes, from Genesis to Revelation God seeks, woos, and pleads with us to come spend time with Him.

Other Messengers/Functions of Prophets

Have our Bibles today included all of God's revelations? Clearly the answer is no. First Chronicles 29:29 and 2 Chronicles 9:29 mention the "book of Nathan the prophet," "the prophecy of Ahijah the Shilonite," and "the visions of Iddo the seer." Second Chronicles 12:15 tells us about "the book of Shemaiah the prophet." We have none of these writings in our current Bible. But 2 Timothy 3:16 and 2 Peter 1:20, 21 tell us that the Holy Spirit has inspired our Scriptures and that we can trust that God saw to it that they contain all that we need for salvation.

Various terms describe the messages given by the prophets: *counsel* (Isa. 44:26), *Lord's message* (Haggai 1:13), *prophecies* (2 Chron. 9:29; 15:8); *testimonies* (1 Kings 2:3; 2 Kings 11:12); and *word of God* (1 Sam. 9:27; 1 Kings 12:22). Through His prophets the Lord reaches out to human beings, seeking ways to explain His will so that we can learn how to walk with Him.

He Sent Jesus Christ

Have you heard of William (Bill) Lishman from Canada? Beginning in 1988, and again in 1990, 1993, 1994, and 1995, he used an ultralight aircraft to lead flocks of Canada geese in their migration. In his first flight he guided 18 geese 400 miles. On his 1995 flight he and a photographer conducted a larger flock of geese more than 800 miles from Ontario to Virginia. How did they accomplish such a feat? In essence, they first had to learn to think like a bird, and then "become a bird" with their ultralight aircraft.

They sought to help preserve a flock of geese. How much greater was Christ's actually becoming a human and coming down to our world to save us from sin! His motivation? Love. Not only did He *think* like us, He literally *became* one of us! "And the Word became flesh and dwelt among us, and we beheld His glory, the glory as of the only begotten of the Father; full of grace and truth" (John 1:14, NKJV).

11

People who lived in the time of Christ expected power above poverty, majesty instead of meekness, when the Messiah would appear in our world. However, the coming of Jesus portrayed the true character of God the Father. Jesus fully revealed God because only He knows the Father (Matt. 11:27). He said to Philip, "He who has seen Me has seen the Father" (John 14:9, NKJV). John 14:8-12 teaches us that those who encountered Him should have learned the nature of the Father, because Jesus and the Father are in each other. Their intimate relationship is much more than that of a master and a disciple. The words that Jesus speaks are more than those of a mere human being—they are a revelation of the actions of God Himself. Therefore, when we become acquainted with Jesus, we have become acquainted with God as well. Although Jesus entered our world in a different form than people expected, His life and teaching demonstrated to humanity the will and love of God. Lishman succeeded in his mission when he thought and "lived" like the geese. He came to know them personally. The best way for us to know Jesus' love and His goodness is to know Him personally by thinking His thoughts and "living" as He did.

Though He had "humbled Himself to humanity, the Godhead was still His own. Christ alone could represent the Father to humanity, and this representation the disciples were privileged to behold for over three years."[1]

What are the things about Jesus that we need to learn? We must come to know Him as intimately as Lishman did his geese. It means that we need to experience Him as the *Word of God* (John 1:1, 2), the world's *Creator* (John 1:3, 10, 11), the world's *Redeemer* (Heb. 9:12), and *God made flesh* (Heb. 2:14). Happily, we can know far more about God than the birds did about Lishman, who flew with them. Unlike the geese, who felt no love toward Lishman, we can love God, and feel His love for us.

Jesus revealed God. "In all that he says and does God is speaking through him. If they [Jesus' listeners] have not the spiritual perception to read the revelation in his whole conduct, if they cannot hear the divine voice in his message, at least they ought to be able to know and understand the 'signs' discernible in His mighty *works*. These tell that *the Father is in me and I am in the father* (John 10:38)."[2]

Kenneth Scott Latourette, a church historian, says, "As the centuries pass, the evidence is accumulating that, measured by his effect on history, Jesus is the most influential life ever lived on this planet. That influence appears to be mounting."[3]

God Speaks to Us Today

God has searched for men and women throughout every age because His enduring love has never given up! He is even more persistent than were those separated by Hurricanes Katrina and Rita. God's seeking differs from the methods employed by the hurricane survivors. They used the Internet, TV, voice messages, and newspaper notices. God cannot turn to such media. Because of sin we cannot see Him face to face, so He constantly seeks us through the Holy Spirit in order that we may find happiness in His presence again.

How does He reveal Himself? Besides revelations through Jesus and the prophets, Paul wrote in Hebrews 1:1 that He spoke to human beings "many times and in many ways" (TEV). The Bible gives several avenues in which He communicates His will to us:

1. God reveals Himself in nature. How often have you gazed deep into the throat of an orchid, or stood transfixed as you watched a blazing sun sink into the ocean, leaving the sky awash with glorious colors? Psalm 19 describes this kind of communication from God: "The heavens declare the glory of God; and the firmament shows His handiwork" (Ps. 19:1, NKJV). Job said, "But ask now the beasts, and they will teach you; and the birds of the air, and they will tell you; or speak to the earth, and it will teach you; and the fishes of the sea will explain to you" (Job 12:7, 8, NKJV).

2. God reveals Himself through the Holy Spirit, who makes contact with each person's conscience. Doubtless you have had times you felt the Holy Spirit impressing you, or guiding you, or comforting you. First Corinthians 2:10 says, "But God has revealed them to us through His Spirit" (NKJV). In John 14:16-18 Jesus said, "I will pray the Father, and He will give you another Helper, that He may abide with you forever. . . . I will not leave you orphans; I will come to you" (NKJV).

3. God reveals Himself through parents and other human relationships. Don't you love to watch a mother with her baby? Long before that infant can understand the meaning of her words, that infant feels the strength of a mother's love. And when parents pray with their children, they are powerfully influencing their little ones. Paul says in 2 Timothy 1:5: "I have been reminded of your sincere faith, which first lived in your grandmother Lois and in your mother Eunice and, I am persuaded, now lives in you also" (NIV).

4. God reveals His will through His servants. A story tells of a Chinese minister imprisoned with many of his believers in a filthy prison camp. No one wanted to clean the latrines or carry the refuse to the fields. But when they saw their pastor carrying bucketful after bucketful of human waste, they more fully understood the role Jesus took in humbling Himself. Philippians 4:2-9 states: "The things which you learned and received and heard, and saw in me, these do, and the God of peace will be with you" (NKJV).

5. *God reveals Himself through His providence.* Nearly all Christians can point to at least one and often dozens of providential experiences in their walk with Jesus. Sometimes such circumstances involve great suffering or uncertainty, and then suddenly they know the answer to their problem or the decision they must make. Psalm 107:6, 7 declares, "Then they cried out to the Lord in their trouble, and He delivered them out of their distresses. And He led them forth by the right way that they might go to a city for a dwelling place" (NKJV).

6. *God reveals Himself through Scripture.* Have you ever had the experience of getting a sudden "Aha!" as you were reading the Bible? Or of finding the answer to some problem right there in Scripture? John 5:39 states: "You search the Scriptures, for in them you think you have eternal life; and these are they which testify of Me" (NKJV). Scripture can guide us in our Christian walk.

How Scripture Came to Us

Many people wonder how the Bible came to be. When God could no longer talk face to face with His children, Adam told the stories to Seth, and Seth shared them with his son. For many years people handed down God's revelations from generation to generation as oral tradition. "The word of the Lord came unto Abram" (Gen. 15:1). While it might have been sufficient for a number of generations, eventually the human race needed something more. Moses was the first person to write the words we now have in the Bible. For example, "Moses wrote all the words of the Lord" (Ex. 24:4; see also Ex. 34:27; Lev. 26:46). The Lord gave specific instruction to him: "Write this for a memorial in the book and recount it in the hearing of Joshua" (Ex. 17:14, NKJV). On another occasion the Bible says, "Now Moses wrote down the starting points of their journeys at the command of the Lord" (Num. 33:2, NKJV). His writings became known as the "book of the law" (Deut. 31:26).

Tradition suggests that Samuel may have been the first person to begin collecting and organizing the writings of Moses. In his schools of the prophets his students copied portions of Scripture to use in teaching the people of Israel. Samuel also did some writing of his own to contribute to the collection (1 Sam. 10:25).

14

Moses wrote in the wilderness, Jeremiah in a dungeon, David on a hill-side or in a palace, Paul from prison, Luke while traveling, and John while exiled on Patmos. The Bible speaks about the prophetic activity of such individuals as Jeremiah (Jer. 36:2), Daniel (Dan. 9:2; 12:4), and many others. Peter describes Paul's writing as "Scriptures" (2 Peter 3:16, NKJV). The Holy Spirit inspired all those who composed the Scriptures (2 Peter 1:21). From their compiled writing the "canon," or "Bible," came into being.

The word "Bible" derives from the Latin word *biblia,* signifying "little books," which originates from the Greek *byblos,* also indicating a book. Thus the expression "holy Bible" means holy *books.* This is very appropriate, because the Bible consists of many books—39 Old Testament books and 27 New Testament ones, totaling 66 in all.

"The theme of God's love, particularly as seen in Christ's sacrificial death on Calvary—the grandest truth of the universe—is the focus of the Bible. All major Bible truths, therefore, should be studied from this perspective."[4]

"Through the Scriptures the Holy Spirit speaks to the mind, and impresses truth upon the heart."[5] "We must place a higher value than we have upon the Scriptures, for therein is the revealed will of God to men. It is not enough merely to assent to the truthfulness of God's Word, but we must search the Scriptures to learn what they contain. Do we receive the Bible as 'the oracle of God'? It is as really a divine communication as though its words came to us in an audible voice."[6]

Jesus said of the Old Testament Scriptures, "These are they which testify of Me" (John 5:39, NKJV). "The whole Bible tells of Christ. From the first record of Creation . . . to the closing promise, 'Behold, I come quickly,' we are reading of His works and listening to His voice."[7]

Josh McDowell quotes Norman Geisler and William Nix when he speaks about the impact of the Bible upon civilization: "The influence of the Bible and its teaching in the Western world is clear for all who study history. And the influential role of the West in the course of world events is equally clear. Civilization has been influenced more by the Judeo-Christian Scriptures than by any other book or series of books in the world. Indeed, no great moral or religious work in the world exceeds the depth of morality in the principle of Christian love, and none has a more lofty spiritual concept than the biblical view of God. The Bible presents the highest ideals known to men, ideals that have molded civilization."[8]

Summary

We can trust the Bible as God's revelation and will for our lives. When you buy a new car, it comes with an owner's manual, written by the creator of the car, that tells you what maintenance it needs, how to troubleshoot problems, and the general care you must provide it. In His love God gave us an owner's manual, the Bible. God intended that men and women be certain regarding the purpose of life and truth, and how to obtain salvation. God has revealed Himself through nature, the Bible, Jesus, divine providence in our lives, human relationships, and the influence of the Holy Spirit. Trusting His revelation through the Scripture can strengthen our faith and bring us into obedience to Him.

We believe the Bible is the expression of God's will in our lives because it reveals the character of the deity who reaches out to human beings for their salvation. In His marvelous love He seeks us through every method available, for He is "patient with you, not wanting anyone to perish, but everyone to come to repentance" (2 Peter 3:9, NIV). Because of our belief, we wrote this book to help you grow in your love of the Bible and in your personal walk with Jesus, the author of this marvelous owner's manual.

---

[1] Ellen G. White, *The Desire of Ages* (Mountain View, Calif.: Pacific Press Pub. Assn., 1898), p. 664.

[2] *The Interpreter's Bible* (Nashville: Abingdon Press, 1952), vol. 8, pp. 634, 635.

[3] In *American Historical Review,* January 1949.

[4] *Seventh-day Adventists Believe* (Washington, D.C.: Ministerial Association, General Conference of Seventh-day Adventists, 1988), pp. 6, 7.

[5] White, *The Desire of Ages,* p. 671.

[6] Ellen G. White, *Testimonies for the Church* (Mountain View, Calif.: Pacific Press Pub. Assn., 1948), vol. 5, p. 533.

[7] Ellen G. White, *Steps to Christ* (Mountain View, Calif.: Pacific Press Pub. Assn., 1956), p. 88.

[8] In Josh McDowell, *The New Evidence That Demands a Verdict* (Nashville: Thomas Nelson Publishers, 1999), p. 15.

CHAPTER 2

The Bible Is Authoritative

Children are famous for trying to play one parent off the other. However, in a stable home the mother will tell the children, "Daddy said no, and that's all there is to discuss." Or the father will announce, "You heard your mother. Now go do it!" Children who recognize that Mommy and Daddy's word is final save themselves from the wheedling and pouting that so emotionally drains the whole family. Why? Because they recognize authority when they hear it. If the parents are fair-minded, parental authority offers a wonderful environment for children to grow in.

In today's society children may have three or four parent figures, and they can become very confused if these various "parents" disagree with each other. Especially is this so if the adults come from contrasting backgrounds. One parent might be a professional, another a day laborer, and still another a stay-at-home parent. Children quickly learn to equate education with wisdom, and often they respect the learned parent over the unlettered one.

We could compare the Bible to some 40 different "parents" (or writers), who came from all walks of life. Some of these writers produced many books. Paul wrote 14 (assuming that he composed Hebrews), John authored five, and Solomon three. Bible writers include fishermen, shepherds, a physician, a prime minister, a king, youth and old age, military leaders, philosophers, priests, musicians, and others. Yet through God's inspiration, each one expressed His words, for "prophecy never came by the will of man, but holy men of God spoke as they were moved by the Holy Spirit" (2 Peter 1:21, NKJV). Because they were inspired, their messages and the compilation of their writings make the Bible God's book, not theirs. It was His words on their tongues; His messages that came from their pens. Amazingly, though the Bible was written by so many people, unity and harmony exist, and a consistent authority emerges.

Ellen White said that Jesus "taught that the Word of God was to be understood by all. He pointed to the Scriptures as of unquestionable authority, and we should do the same. The Bible is to be presented as the word of the infinite God, as the end of all controversy and the foundation of all faith."[1]

The Authorship of the Bible

You can find books today composed of chapters by different authors. But have you ever encountered a book written by 40 different authors that "hangs together" as a cohesive unit? And have you ever read a book (other than the Bible) written during a period of 1,500 years that is still relevant today and that does not contradict itself? How did the Bible achieve this? Its writers claimed to receive their messages from divine sources rather than conjuring up their own ideas. The biblical authors repeatedly used several phrases to describe the sources of their messages: "The Lord has spoken" (Isa. 1:2, NKJV). "This is what the Lord says" (Amos 1:3, NKJV). "The word of the Lord that came to . . ." (Micah 1:1, NKJV). Or: "This is what the Lord has revealed to me" (Jer. 38:21, NIV). Clearly God is the real author. Most of the Bible writers pointed to the Holy Spirit as the one who communicated through the prophets and apostles to the people.

If you consult a Bible concordance, you will find more than 300 statements basically stating "The Lord spoke unto Moses" in the first five books of the Bible alone!

The Bible has made no direct attempt to prove God's assistance in its writings. It assumes it. More than a thousand times Old Testament writers claimed the Lord as the authority for what they wrote (see Amos 3:1 and Joshua 1:1). New Testament writers either quoted directly from the Old Testament or gave allusions to specific verses found in the Old Testament, and, like their predecessors, they acknowledged God as their source (see Luke 1:70; Rom. 4:3; Gal. 1:11, 12).

Yes, the Bible is the Word of God, given by His will through His prophets and apostles. And the point is this: since no higher authority than God Himself can exist, the Bible has authority in our lives.

Inspired by God

But *how* did these prophets receive their messages? Second Timothy 3:16 answers the question: "All scripture is given by inspiration of God." The Greek word *theopneustos* here literally means "God-*breathed*," indicating that the Scripture originated from God. He moved His messengers, prophets, and apostles to understand and then communicate that which He revealed to them. Interestingly, it was through the *breath* of God that He created human beings (Gen. 2:7), and it was through the divine *breath* that the universe came into existence (Ps. 33:6). The power of this same creative *breath* also brought the Scriptures into being.

Whatever method the Holy Spirit employed to communicate His messages (dreams, visions, spoken words, etc.), it's important to understand that the writers of the Bible were not merely automatic writing machines. God did not use them like keys on a typewriter to produce His messages. The prophets themselves had the right to express in their own words the things He told them. Thus the Bible is not the product of mere mechanical dictation. Each prophet chose culturally appropriate words and images so that the men and women of his age could understand the divine message. Each writer used his own individual writing style. Ellen White comments, "The writers of the Bible were God's penmen, not His pen."[2]

The prophets consciously spoke as God's mouthpieces. "The Spirit of the Lord spoke through me; his word was on my tongue" (2 Sam. 23:2, NIV). The Bible says in Jeremiah 1:9, "Then the Lord . . . said to me, 'Now, I have put my words in your mouth'" (NIV). Amos 3:8 announces: "The Sovereign Lord has spoken—who can but prophesy?" (NIV). Such individuals were not speaking on their own initiative. Energized by God, they were under the guidance of the Holy Spirit in whatever they said or wrote. Notice some of the ways Scripture refers to itself:

book of the Lord	Isaiah 34:16
gospel of God	Romans 1:1
oracles of God	Romans 3:2
good word of God	Hebrews 6:5
word of Christ	Colossians 3:16

Benjamin Warfield, in his book *Revelation and Inspiration,* comments: "The men who spoke from God are here declared, therefore, to have been taken up by the Holy Spirit and brought by His power to the goal of His choosing. The things which they spoke under this operation of the Spirit were therefore His things, not theirs. And that is the reason which is assigned why 'the prophetic word' is so sure. Though spoken through the instrumentality of men, it is, by virtue of the fact that these men spoke as 'borne by the Holy Spirit,' an immediately Divine word."[3]

Ellen White supported this. "Patriarchs, prophets, and apostles spoke as they were moved upon by the Holy Ghost, and they plainly stated that they spoke not by their own power, nor in their own name. . . . They were jealous for the honor of God, to whom all praise belongs. They declared that their ability and the messages they brought were given them as delegates of the power of God. God was the authority and sufficiency."[4]

Christ's View of the Scriptures

Jesus had this same high view of the Bible. Whether talking with Satan, Pharisees, or Sadducees, He consistently used Scripture as His authority to rebuke or refute. Notice in the sidebar Jesus' references to things in the Old Testament, showing His familiarity to it and His acceptance of it as the authoritative Word of God.

Abel (Luke 11:51)
Noah (Matt. 24:37-39; Luke 17:26, 27)
Abraham (John 8:56)
the practice of circumcision (John 7:22)
Sodom and Gomorrah (Matt. 10:15; 11:23, 24; Luke 10:12)
Lot (Luke 17:28-32)
Isaac and Jacob (Matt. 8:11; Luke 13:28)
manna (John 6:31, 49, 58)
wilderness serpent (John 3:14)
David eating the shewbread (Matt. 12:3, 4; Mark 2:25, 26; Luke 6:3, 4)
David as a psalm writer (Matt. 22:43; Mark 12:36; Luke 20:42)
Solomon (Matt. 6:29; 12:42; Luke 11:31; 12:27)
Elijah (Luke 4:25, 26)
Elisha (Luke 4:27)
Jonah (Matt. 12:39-41; Luke 11:29, 30, 32)
Zechariah (Luke 11:51)

Jesus also made repeated allusions to Moses as the giver of the law (Matt. 8:4; 19:8; Mark 1:44; 7:10; 10:3-5; 12:26; Luke 5:14; 20:37; John 5:46; 7:19). He frequently mentioned the sufferings of the prophets (Matt. 5:12; 13:57; 21:34-36; 23:29-37; Mark 6:4; 12:2-5; Luke 6:23; 11:47-51; 13:34: 20:10-12). And He showed His belief in the story of Creation (Matt. 19:4, 5; Mark 10:6-8).

Every organized country of the world can point to its constitution as the final authority for legal questions. The document serves as the nation's "compass." As long as the citizens abide by its principles, they live in peace. Jesus gave the Old Testament writings the same authority as a constitution and taught people to live by its principles. Of course, at the heart of this "constitution" are the Ten Commandments, and Jesus rebuked people who did not obey the divine law. He scolded the scribes and Pharisees and told the people to "practice and observe whatever they tell you, but not what they do; for they preach, but do not practice" (Matt. 23:3, RSV). When answering a question posed to Him by the Sadducees, He said, "You are in error because you do not know the Scriptures or the power of God" (Matt. 22:29, NIV).

Again, when a lawyer asked which was the greatest commandment, Jesus supported the authority of the Scripture by quoting from two Old Testament verses urging the people to love the Lord with all their hearts and their neighbor as themselves (Deut. 6:5; Lev. 19:18). He summarized by saying, "The whole Law of Moses and the teachings of the prophets depend on these two commandments" (Matt. 22:40, TEV).

Put yourself in Jesus' place when the devil tried to tempt Him. How would you have responded? Jesus used Scripture, saying, "It is written." The Greek actually means "It stands written," showing that Jesus understood the words of the Bible to be equivalent to "God says." Jesus recognized Moses, David, Isaiah, and other Bible writers as inspired with messages given by the Holy Spirit (Mark 7:6, 10; 12:36).

As He sat teaching the Sermon on the Mount, Jesus showed His acceptance of Scripture as the final authority by saying, "Not an iota, not a dot, will pass from the law" (Matt. 5:18, RSV). He used the Creation story to support marriage (Gen. 2:24, quoted in Matt. 19:5). What scriptures do you think He employed when talking with the two travelers on the road to Emmaus and later the disciples? We know that He used "Moses and all the Prophets" as He "expounded to them in all the Scriptures the things concerning Himself" (Luke 24:27, NKJV; see also verses 44-47).

We can see that throughout His life Jesus spoke from, promoted, uplifted, and interpreted the Bible. As Hans LaRondelle aptly states:

"Jesus is the true Interpreter of Holy Scripture. His message is our key to unlock the correct meaning of the Old Testament. . . . Christ's use of Israel's Scriptures is our model of biblical interpretation. Our guiding principle is based on the conviction that the redemptive activity of God in the history of Israel reached its fulfillment in Christ."[5]

The Apostles and Scripture

All the apostles believed in and quoted extensively from the only Bible they had. Compare these three columns to learn how they supported Scripture.

Apostles' Statement	New Testament Text	Old Testament Text
admonition to rich	James 1:11	Isaiah 40:6, 7 Psalm 103:15
a lamb without blemish	1 Peter 1:19	Exodus 12:5
man's sinful nature	Romans 3:10–12	Psalm 14:1–3
creation of universe	John 1:3 Colossians 1:16, 17	Genesis 1
creation of Adam and Eve	1 Timothy 2:13, 14	Genesis 1; 2
temptation of Eve	1 Timothy 2:14	Genesis 3
disobedience, sin of Adam	Romans 5:12 1 Corinthians 15:22	Genesis 3
sacrifices of Cain and Abel	Hebrews 11:4	Genesis 4
Cain murders Abel	1 John 3:12	Genesis 4
Enoch translated	Hebrews 11:5	Genesis 5
marriage before the Flood	Luke 17:27	Genesis 6
call of Abraham	Luke 3:34	Genesis 12; 13
justification of Abraham	Romans 4:3	Genesis 15
miracles of Elijah	James 5:17	1 Kings 17; 18

You recognize, of course, that this is only a smattering of the New Testament writers' use of the Old Testament as they composed the New Testament. In the book of Romans alone Paul referred directly to the Old Testament more than 40 times. Peter, James, and John likewise cited extensively from the Hebrew Scriptures. The book of Revelation is filled with references to the Old Testament.

Supernatural Unity

Rather than being an ordinary book, the Bible is a library composed of 66 individual works. We have already noted the many different kinds of people who wrote them. They lived in different countries and on three continents (Africa, Asia, and Europe), and their lives spanned some 1,600 years. Yet all of them spoke about the same God who loves intensely. Although the writers of the Bible came from such diversified backgrounds and places, a unity of purpose emerges in a single unfolding story of God's searching love and His plan to rescue human beings.

"Unity is one of the clearly recognized characteristics of the Scriptures.

There is unity of purpose—the story of the plan of salvation. There is unity in its theme—Jesus Christ, His cross and His crown. There is complete harmony of teaching—the doctrines of the Old Testament and those of the New are the same. There is unity of development—a steady progression from the Creation to the Fall and onto the redemption and the final restoration. There is unity in the coordination of the prophecies. How can it be? The same Spirit who spoke through Moses spoke 16 centuries later through John the revelator. And in all the centuries between, that same Spirit testified of the same Father-God and the same Messiah, and the same plan for mankind."[6]

The New Testament enlarges on various Old Testament themes:

- The Ten Commandments are clearly explained by the Sermon on the Mount.
- Isaiah's prophecies are fulfilled in the narrative of the Gospels.
- Leviticus is more clearly understood by studying the Epistle to the Hebrews.
- The Passover foreshadows the Lord's Supper.
- Genesis tells of the first creation while Revelation foretells the new creation.

Consider how amazing it is to find a book with such unity, yet that came from such varied authors and places. Making it even more incredible is the fact that "during the first twenty-five hundred years of human history, there was no written revelation. Those who had been taught of God communicated their knowledge to others, and it was handed down from father to son, through successive generations. The preparation of the Written Word began in the time of Moses. Inspired revelations were then embodied in an inspired book. This work continued during the long period of sixteen hundred years—from Moses, the historian of creation and the law, to John, the recorder of the most sublime truths of the gospel."[7]

Summary

The evidence that the Bible has only one true Author working through many people to proclaim His message of love, His search for His lost children, and His never giving up is overwhelming. We can trust the fully inspired Bible as the infallible, solely authoritative Word of God.

---

[1] Ellen G. White, *Christ's Object Lessons* (Mountain View, Calif.: Pacific Press Pub. Assn., 1900), pp. 39, 40.

[2] Ellen G. White, *Selected Messages* (Washington, D.C.: Review and Herald Pub. Assn., 1958), book 1, p. 21.

[3] Benjamin Warfield, *Revelation and Inspiration* (New York: Oxford University Press, 1927), p. 83.

[4] In *Review and Herald,* Jan. 7, 1890.

[5] Hans LaRondelle, *How to Understand the End-Time Prophecies of the Bible* (Sarasota, Fla.: First Impressions, 1997), p. 13.

[6] T. H. Jemison, *Christian Beliefs* (Mountain View, Calif.: Pacific Press Pub. Assn., 1959), p. 17.

[7] Ellen G. White, *The Great Controversy* (Mountain View, Calif.: Pacific Press Pub. Assn., 1911), p. v.

CHAPTER 3

The Bible's Prophecies Are Fulfilled

What do the following names bring to your mind?

Jeane Dixon

Nostradamus

Edgar Cayce

Ruth Montgomery

All of them claimed to be "psychics." Why did they attract such public interest? They all claimed to predict the future. People seek out those whom they believe can tell them what is coming. Yet studies show that only 4 percent of the predictions of such psychics actually get fulfilled. Four percent? That's hardly an impressive success rate! But people desperately want to know what will happen in the future. What will happen to me? my family? my country? Is this world going to last forever? Do I have a bright future? How many more years will I live? Everything seems so uncertain, and we long for some kind of assurance that things will somehow work out.

Visit a bookstore, and you will find many books related to future predictions. The search engine "Dogpile" revealed approximately 100 entries for both "end time scenario" and "end of world." Some claim that as many as 250 Web sites currently deal with end-time scenarios. People want to know their fate!

Josh McDowell quoted Wilbur Smith in a rather lengthy paragraph. Smith, who compiled a personal library of 25,000 volumes, said that "whatever one may think of the authority of and the message presented in the book we call the Bible, there is a worldwide agreement that in more ways than one it is the most remarkable volume that has ever been produced in these some five thousand years of writing. . . . It is the only volume . . . in which is to be found a large body of prophecies relating to individual nations, to Israel, to all the peoples of the earth, to certain cities, and to the coming of One who was to be Messiah. The ancient world had many different devices for determining the future, know as divination, but not in the entire gamut of Greek and Latin literature . . . can we find any real specific prophecy of a great historic event to come in the distant future, nor any prophecy of a Savior to arise in the human race." [1]

The Benefits of Prophecy

Did God give specific prophecies just to meet our curiosity about the future? Or did He have another purpose in mind? God actually had several good reasons for including predictions of the future in the Bible. Let's consider three of them.

To confirm the prophetic gift. Jesus warned us about false prophets (Matt. 24:24). Therefore it's crucial to determine whether a message comes originally from the Lord or not. The fulfillment of a prophet's prediction can serve as one test of whether the individual is a true prophet. Jeremiah wrote, "But the prophet who prophesies peace will be recognized as one truly sent by the Lord only if his prediction comes true" (Jer. 28:9, NIV). Moses said that the failure of a prediction would show that the message came from a false prophet (Deut. 18:21, 22). For that reason, Paul advises us, "Do not treat prophecies with contempt. Test everything. Hold on to the good" (1 Thess. 5:20, 21, NIV).

W. A. Spicer, an early Adventist pioneer, wrote, "To the Lord, the future is an open book, even as the present. The word is spoken, telling of the event to come; it is written on the parchment scroll by the prophet's pen. Time passes; centuries come and go. Then, when the hour of the prophecy arrives, lo, there appears the fulfillment." [2]

To confirm our faith. As Jesus was leaving the Temple one day, His disciples called attention to its grandeur. But Jesus was not impressed with its grandeur. "I tell you the truth, not one stone will be left on another; every one will be thrown down," He told them (Matt. 24:1, 2, NIV).

Thinking He was speaking of His second coming, the disciples asked, "When will this happen, and what will be the sign of Your coming and of the end of the age?" (verse 3, NIV).

Jesus replied: "Now learn this parable from the fig tree: When its branch has already become tender and puts forth leaves, you know that summer is near. So you also, when you see all these things, know that it is near—at the doors!" (verses 32, 33, NKJV). In John 13:19 He told His disciples, "I am telling you now before it happens, so that when it does happen you will believe that I am He" (NIV). Thus prophecy is not only

26

information about the future. When we see it fulfilled, our faith strengthens and conviction that the Bible really does come from God deepens.

So that we can prepare for what lies ahead. The daily news shouts that the world is in a terrible state. Wars, famines, and fear break out everywhere. The world sinks lower and lower in the mire of sin. No shame surrounds the discussing of multiple affairs. Politicians do not keep their promises to their constituents, nor do employers always treat employees fairly. Pictures in the news show children's starving faces staring at us, begging for food. One part of the earth reels under floods while another part suffers drought. What does all this mean? Where can we turn for hope? If we believe the Bible, we recognize these things as "birth pangs," the "beginning of sorrows" that must precede Jesus' second coming. All this helps us to understand that we are living in the last days.

Knowing that Jesus is returning soon prompts us to search the Scriptures with the question of the jailer in Philippi in mind: "What must I do to be saved?" (Acts 16:30). How can we prepare for the ultimate fulfillment of prophecy—Jesus' second coming? Scripture will guide us as we prepare for that grand event. Only in Scripture can we find reliable counsel specifically designed to help us get ready for what lies ahead.

Kinds of Prophecy

The Bible contains hundreds of prophecies. We will examine four important groups: "Early Predictions," "Predictions of World Kingdoms," "Messianic Prophecies," and "Second Coming Prophecies."

Early predictions. God Himself gave the first prophecy to Adam and Eve in the Garden of Eden after they had sinned. He said, "I will put enmity between you and the woman, and between your offspring and hers; he will crush your head, and you will strike his heel" (Gen. 3:15, NIV). Christian interpreters generally recognize that it is a prediction of the coming of the Messiah.

Another early prediction was that of the Flood, foretold to Noah (Gen. 6:13, 14), a prophecy fulfilled 120 years later. Jesus obviously believed the story of the Flood, as did the writer of the book of Hebrews (Luke 17:27; Heb. 11:7).

God gave Abraham several prophecies. The first was that he would become a great nation (Gen. 12:1-3). The Israelites grew into a great people in Egypt, and God presented them their national laws at Mount Sinai. They physically established themselves as a nation when they invaded the land of Canaan and drove out its numerous pagan inhabitants. With the exception of the 70 years of Babylonian captivity, the Jews continued to exist as a nation until shortly after Christ's death and resurrection.

Abraham's near sacrifice of his son also gave him light concerning the future and helped him understand Jesus' role in saving sinners. "By faith he saw the world's Redeemer coming as God in the flesh. He saw the weight of guilt lifted from the human race, and borne by the divine substitute."[3]

Finally, God told the patriarch about the slavery his descendants would experience in Egypt and their deliverance 430 years later. The last part of Genesis and the first five chapters of Exodus dramatically show the fulfillment of that prophecy when Moses led the Hebrews out of Egypt.

Predictions of world kingdoms. Just as you and I want to know the future, King Nebuchadnezzar, the ruler of Babylon, also sought to learn his destiny. You are familiar with the story of the dream the king had and how Daniel told him what he had seen and then interpreted it. The prophet explained that "there is a God in heaven who reveals mysteries" (Dan. 2:28, NIV).

Nebuchadnezzar's kingdom was the head of gold, followed by inferior kingdoms: Medo-Persia, the breast and arms of silver; Greece, the belly and thighs of brass; and Rome, the legs of iron. Daniel then predicted the emergence of even lesser nations, symbolized by feet of iron mixed with clay. Finally, a stone "cut out . . . without hands" (Dan. 2:45, NIV) would strike the image and totally destroy it. The stone would then enlarge and fill the whole world.

World history supports the accuracy of this prediction. Babylon was the dominant power in the Middle East at Nebuchadnezzar's time. Today the ruins of the city of Babylon sprawl in the land of Iraq, 70 miles south of Baghdad. The Bible had predicted a curse on Babylon (Isa. 13), and its fall (Jer. 51:49, 53). Isaiah announced that Cyrus's army would attack and conquer the city: "This is what the Lord says to his anointed, to Cyrus, whose right hand I take hold of . . . to open doors before him so that gates will not be shut: I will go before you and will level the mountains; I will break down gates of bronze and cut through bars of iron" (Isa. 45:1, 2, NIV). History records the amazing fulfillment of this prophecy more than 150 years later, when the Medo-Persian army lowered the waters of the Euphrates River, marched under the walls of Babylon, and entered its opened gates while King Belshazzar and nobles celebrated a great feast.

The story continued in Daniel 2:39 with a third kingdom of bronze that would rule the biblical world. Daniel 8:21 stated that Greece would follow Medo-Persia. In fulfillment of the prediction, the Greek armies, led by Alexander the Great, conquered the Medo-Persian Empire wearing bronze breastplates and helmets and carrying bronze shields and swords.

History tells us that Rome, symbolized by the legs of iron, conquered Greece during the second century B.C. Rome had a longer dominion than any of the other ancient kingdoms, ruling the Mediterranean world for more than 500 years. However, Daniel said that the Roman Empire (the legs of iron) "will be a divided kingdom" (Dan. 2:41, NIV). The empire fell and broke into numerous independent kingdoms that eventually evolved into the modern nations surrounding the Mediterranean Sea. Today we live in the time of the feet of clay, and the stone is likely to strike the image on the feet at any time. We believe that Jesus is coming very soon.

Besides that of Daniel 2, we find many other prophecies involving ancient kingdoms that have seen fulfillment. Consider the following:

the destruction of Edom (Obadiah);

the destruction of Tyre (Eze. 26) and Nineveh (Nahum);

the return of Israel to the Promised Land (Isa. 11:11).

Such fulfilled prophecies indicate the divine authority of the Bible.

Messianic prophecies. The early apostles frequently quoted Old Testament prophecies to show that Jesus' birth, life, and death had fulfilled them precisely. Paul demonstrated from the Old Testament scriptures that "according to the prophecies and the universal expectation of the Jews, the Messiah would be of the lineage of Abraham and of David; then he traced the descent of Jesus from the patriarch Abraham through the royal psalmist. He read the testimony of the prophets regarding the character and work of the promised Messiah, and His reception and treatment on the earth; then he showed that all these predictions had been fulfilled in the life, ministry, and death of Jesus of Nazareth."[4]

Messianic prophecies appear throughout the Old Testament, and they constitute powerful evidence of the divine origin of the Bible. On page 30 are a number of messianic prophecies and their fulfillments.

The Old Testament has numerous prophecies regarding Jesus' birth, life, death, and resurrection. They are full of contingencies that could not have been rigged in advance to arrange their fulfillment. Not until after Jesus' final 40 days with His disciples, following His ascension, did they begin to sense how the prophecies had met their fulfillments. The scenes of the crucifixion, resurrection, and ascension of Christ were a living reality to them, as they recognized how each had pointed forward to Jesus. "They searched the Scriptures, and accepted their teaching with a faith and assurance unknown before. They knew that the divine Teacher was all that He had claimed to be."[5]

Jesus Himself referred to the predictions about Him. He told two

Prophecy	Old Testament Source	New Testament Fulfillment
a prophet like Moses	Deuteronomy 18:18, 19	Acts 3:17-24
the suffering victim	Psalm 22 Isaiah 53:7, 8	John 19:18-24
the virgin birth	Isaiah 7:14	Matthew 1:22, 23
the divine-human king	Isaiah 9:6, 7	Luke 22:30 John 18:36, 37
the time of His coming	Daniel 9:24	Galatians 4:4
the place of His birth	Micah 5:2	Matthew 2:1
a forerunner of Messiah	Isaiah 40:3	John 1:19-23
the killing of infants in Bethlehem	Jeremiah 31:15	Matthew 2:16
the flight to Egypt	Hosea 11:1	Matthew 2:14
as the Rock of Offense	Isaiah 8:14; 28:16	Romans 9:32, 33
His rejection	Isaiah 53:3	Matthew 27:22, 23 John 1:11
His victory	Isaiah 53:12	Matthew 12:20 Revelation 3:21

disciples on the road to Emmaus, "How foolish you are, and how slow of heart to believe all that the prophets have spoken! Did not the Christ have to suffer these things and then enter his glory? And beginning with Moses and all the Prophets, he explained to them what was said in all the Scriptures concerning Himself" (Luke 24:25-27, NIV). Some of "those things" might have included the above-mentioned texts, plus the following:

His ministry (Isaiah 9:1, 2; Matthew 4:12-16)
being mocked and insulted (Psalm 22:6-8; Matthew 27:39, 40)
being crucified with sinners (Isaiah 53:12; Mathew 27:38)
His resurrection (Psalm 16:10; Matthew 28:9)

When people see the many predictions concerning Christ fulfilled and acknowledge that these things couldn't have just happened, the Holy Spirit draws them to Jesus. The whole purpose of the Bible, including prophecy, is just that—to draw people to Christ.

Prophecies and signs of His second coming. So far, we have studied prophecies that have met their completion in the past. However, the Bible has many predictions involving the future. They relate to the *promise* of His coming, the *signs* of His coming, and the *conditions* in the world just before His return.

Near the close of World War II General Douglas MacArthur, ordered to leave Bataan in the Philippines, fled to Australia. On March 20, 1942, he promised, "I shall return." Prisoners of war clung to that promise. True to his word, he did come back. Likewise, Jesus declared to His disciples in John that "if I go . . . , I will come back" (John 14:3, NIV). Like the prisoners of war, Peter believed Jesus' words. He said, "But in keeping with his promise we are looking forward to a new heaven and a new earth" (2 Peter 3:13, NIV).

We find many prophecies concerning the second coming of Jesus. Notice the following:

the manner of Christ's return	Acts 1:11; Matthew 24:27, 30
the righteous dead at His return	1 Thessalonians 4:16, 17
the righteous living at His return	1 Corinthians 15:53
unbelievers at His return	Revelation 6:16, 17
false messiahs prior to His return	Matthew 24:4, 5
wars and rumors of war	Matthew 24:6, 7
famine	Matthew 24:7
pestilence	Luke 21:11
earthquakes	Matthew 24:7
social problems	2 Timothy 3:1-5
people living in fear	Luke 21:26
economic problems	James 5:1-5
increased skepticism	2 Peter 3:3, 4
fragile peace	1 Thessalonians 5:3
gospel preached to whole world	Matthew 24:14

Back in 1956 Doris Day popularized the song "Que Sera, Sera"—Spanish words that in English mean "Whatever will be, will be." The song raises the question we all ask: What does my future hold? Few people claim to be capable of predicting the future, but the Bible confidently tells what lies thousands of years ahead. No book, other than the Bible, has shown the ability to predict so accurately. Having seen that so many of these prophecies have come to pass, we can easily trust the truthfulness of the rest of the Bible.

Summary

As we contemplate the fulfilled prophecies regarding the Flood, the rise and fall of major kingdoms and powers, and the coming of the Messiah, we can trace divine inspiration at work. We look at the signs predicting Jesus' return and recognize that most of them have already materialized. Our confidence in the Bible grows as we recognize the surety of its predictions. We can be positive that those prophecies that yet remain unfilled will soon be realized.

Prophecy assures us that we can know the future! God's love letter, His "owner's manual," promises forgiveness, salvation, and eternal life with Jesus. What a solid foundation we have, one that offers us hope and certainty. Let us resolve to study His Word each day, in order to learn more about what we must do to prepare for the final events of history.

---

[1] In Josh McDowell, *The New Evidence That Demands a Verdict,* p. 12.

[2] W. A. Spicer, *Our Day in the Light of Prophecy* (Washington, D.C.: Review and Herald Pub. Assn., 1917), p. 26.

[3] *The Seventh-day Adventist Bible Commentary,* Ellen G. White Comments (Washington, D.C.: Review and Herald Pub. Assn., 1953), vol. 1, p. 1092.

[4] Ellen G. White, *The Acts of the Apostles* (Mountain View, Calif.: Pacific Press Pub. Assn., 1911), p. 247.

[5] White, *The Desire of Ages,* p. 667.

CHAPTER 4

The Bible Is Reliable

The full-page color ad in the May 26, 2006, edition of the New York Times arrested my attention. In red capital letters on a black background it said: "#1 MOVIE IN THE WORLD." The second line, about an inch below, in white letters against the still-black background, asked: "WHAT DO YOU BELIEVE?" The ad also listed all the places *The Da Vinci Code* movie would play in New York City.

Probably equally as important a question as "What do you believe?" is *"Why* do you believe what you believe?"

Many Christians wring their hands in anguish over the untruths presented as facts in Dan Brown's fictional book *The Da Vinci Code,* on which the movie is based. Sadly, millions have accepted Hollywood's version of Scripture and history and have rejected Christianity.

In strong protest against Dan Brown's untruths, scholars from many different disciplines united in providing historical evidence that counters the supposed facts portrayed in the book and on the screen.

What reason, then, do Christians have for believing the Bible? Thankfully, both internal and external evidence exists to sustain our belief in Scripture. This chapter will look at both. The next chapter will consider even more external evidence.

Perhaps we should first define the two terms *internal evidence* and *external evidence.* A recent radio talk show host quoted some Army officer as saying that President George Bush was "the most stubborn man I have ever known." That's external evidence, because the Army officer is outside the president's immediate family. But suppose the president's wife, Laura, declared, "My husband is the most stubborn man I have ever known." That would be internal evidence, because she's a part of his immediate family.

External evidence includes such things as history, archaeology, and documents written by nonbiblical writers or the testimony of a modern person's experience regarding the power of Scripture on his or her life. Such witnesses to the Bible's reliability are all outside of the Bible. That's why we call them external evidence.

On the other hand, when we quote something from Scripture to support its reliability (such as Paul's statement that "all Scripture is given by inspiration of God" [2 Tim. 3:16, NKJV]), we are using internal evidence, because the Bible is testifying about itself.

Christians are sometimes accused of using circular reasoning when they give internal evidence to substantiate their faith in the Bible. Reasoning is circular when the premise and the proof of the premise are the same thing. For example, it's circular reasoning to say, "Ice cream is my favorite dessert because I like it." The premise (ice cream is my favorite dessert) and the proof of the premise (because I like it) are the same thing. Christians do this when they say, "The Bible is inspired because it says so."

It's important to understand that this kind of reasoning has its place. It's OK for me to say, "I like ice cream just because I like it." I'm my own best evidence for my preferences. And it's OK for Christians to say, "The Bible is inspired because it says so." That's internal evidence, and it's appropriate to use internal evidence in certain situations.

In this chapter we're going to examine both internal and external evidence of the Bible's reliability. We'll start with the Old Testament, and then we'll look at the New Testament.

A Reliable Old Testament

Many biblical scholars tend to analyze the Bible the way they would any other piece of literature. While there's a place for that, it's easy in the process to come to think of the Bible as just another ancient document. As Christians we believe that the Bible is *more* than ordinary literature. God inspired it. So what internal and external evidences can we find that would lead us to accept the Old Testament as His word and not just a product of human wisdom?

Internal evidence. The Old Testament testifies to its inspiration by God. One of the best known examples is Isaiah 8:20. The prophet wrote, "To the law and to the testimony: if they speak not according to this word, it is because there is no light in them."

Many times the Bible writers testified that they proclaimed God's word:

- Moses told Pharaoh, "This is what the Lord says: Let my people go" (Ex. 8:20, NIV).

- "The word of the Lord that came to Joel" (Joel 1:1, NIV).
- "The word of the Lord came to the prophet Zechariah" (Zech. 1:1, NIV).

The Old Testament prophets insisted that what they said was reliable because they were speaking words that they had received from God. Moses claimed that God gave Him the Ten Commandments. Jeremiah acknowledged, "When your words came, I ate them; they were my joy and my heart's delight" (Jer. 15:16, NIV). Even Balaam, who rebelled against God, admitted that he could "speak only what God puts in my mouth" (Num. 22:38, NIV). And Paul, referring to the Old Testament, said that "all Scripture is given by inspiration of God" (2 Tim. 3:16, NKJV), for it was from the Old Testament that he and the other apostles demonstrated that Jesus was the Messiah.

External evidence. We have abundant external evidence for the reliability of the Old Testament. One excellent line of evidence is the ancient manuscripts of the Bible themselves. The study of such manuscripts, called "textual criticism," is an important part of external evidence. Textual criticism compares the many manuscripts available to determine as nearly as possible what the original manuscripts—those written by the Bible writers themselves—must have said.

For many years we had no complete copies of the Hebrew Old Testament dated earlier than about A.D. 900. Scholars referred to them as the "Masoretic text," because they were the product of a special class of scribes whose sole duty was to preserve and transmit Scripture with perfect fidelity. They used special techniques known as *massora* to maintain the accuracy of Scripture. Among other things, they counted every letter, syllable, word, and paragraph. In this way they safeguarded Scripture in a way that no other ancient manuscript has ever been preserved. "Who ever counted the letters and syllables and words of Plato or Aristotle? Cicero or Seneca?"[1]

But what about the accuracy and authenticity of the Old Testament in pre-Masoretic times? At certain periods the history of the Jews was very turbulent, raising a question in the minds of modern scholars as to the carefulness of the scribes during such hectic times. After thousands of years of history, can we still believe in the accuracy of the Old Testament?

The Dead Sea scrolls. In the spring of 1947 Bedouin goat herders, searching the cliffs along the Dead Sea for a lost goat (or for treasure—the story varies), came upon a cave that contained jars filled with manuscripts.

The find caused a sensation when word of it reached the world, and it continues to fascinate the scholarly community and the public.

The discoveries first came to the attention of scholars in 1948, when Bedouins sold seven of the scrolls to Khalil Eskander Shahin, an antiquities dealer popularly known as "Kando." "He in turn sold three of the scrolls to . . . [the] Hebrew University, and four to . . . the Syrian Orthodox monastery of St. Mark." These four were brought "to the American School of Oriental Research, where they came to the attention of American and European scholars."[2]

The discovery included some of the earliest manuscripts yet known of the complete book of Isaiah and fragments of almost every book in the Old Testament. The books of Samuel, in a tattered copy, were also found, along with two complete chapters of Habakkuk. Commenting on the remarkable importance of the scrolls, B. K. Waltke said, "The presence of a text type among the Dead Sea scrolls (c. 200 B.C. to A.D. 100) identical with the one preserved by the Masoretes, whose earliest extant manuscript dates to c. A.D. 900, gives testimony to the unbelievable achievement of some scribes in faithfully preserving the text. Of course, this text must have been in existence before the time of the Dead Sea scrolls, and its many archaic forms in contrast to other text types give strong reason to believe that it was transmitted in a circle of scribes dedicated to the preservation of the original text."[3]

How do the Dead Sea scrolls confirm the reliability of the Old Testament? R. Laird Harris points out that by comparing the Dead Sea scrolls with the Masoretic text of Isaiah 38-66 with the one we had, scholars found that the text is extremely close. "Only 17 letters differ from the Masoretic text. Ten of these are mere differences in spelling, like our 'honor' and [the English] 'honour,' and produce no changes in the meaning at all. Four more are very minor differences, such as the presence of the conjunction, which is often a matter of style. The other three letters are the Hebrew word for 'light' (roa). This word was added to the text by someone after 'they shall see' in verse 11. Out of 166 words in this chapter, only this one word is really in question, and it does not at all change the sense of the passage. This is typical of the whole manuscript."[4]

The Septuagint and the Samaritan Pentateuch. Two other ancient witnesses attest to the accuracy of the copyists who ultimately gave us the Masoretic text. One is the Greek translation of the Old Testament, called the Septuagint (often abbreviated as LXX), and the other is a text preserved by the ancient Samaritan sect called the Samaritan Pentateuch. These three main types of text (Masoretic, Septuagint, and Samaritan), all of which existed in 200 B.C., differ so little among themselves that they confirm the faithful and careful work of earlier copyists.[5] Harris goes on to say, "Indeed, it would be rash skepticism that would now deny that we have our Old Testament in a form very close to that used by Ezra when he taught the Law to those who had returned from the Babylonian captivity."[6]

The Dead Sea scrolls, the Septuagint, the Samaritan Pentateuch, and the Masoretic manuscripts together constitute strong external evidence that the Old Testament is reliable.

A Reliable New Testament

We've already quoted Paul's statement that "all Scripture is given by inspiration of God" (2 Tim. 3:16, NKJV). However, we have a great deal of additional evidence.

Internal evidence. Peter made one of the boldest declarations about the inspiration of the Bible. He stated that "no prophecy of Scripture came about by the prophet's own interpretation. For prophecy never had its origin in the will of man, but men spoke from God as they were carried along by the Holy Spirit" (2 Peter 1:20, 21, NIV). Peter also assured his readers that "we have not followed cunningly devised fables, when we made known unto you the power and coming of our Lord Jesus Christ, but were eyewitnesses of His majesty" (verse 16).

John expressed a similar thought: "That which was from the beginning, which we have heard, which we have seen with our eyes, which we have looked at and our hands have touched—this we proclaim concerning the Word of life" (1 John 1:1, NIV). In Revelation John added, "The revelation of Jesus Christ, which God gave him to show his servants what must soon take place. He made it known by sending his angel to his servant John, who testifies to everything he saw—that is, the word of God and the testimony of Jesus Christ" (Rev. 1:1, 2, NIV).

Paul claimed to have received his teachings through a revelation from God (see Gal. 1:11, 12). And Jesus Himself assured us that He spoke words given to Him by God. "The words I say to you are not just my own. Rather, it is the Father, living in me, who is doing his work" (John 14:10, NIV).

Further internal evidence comes from Luke, who declared, "Many have undertaken to draw up an account of the things that have been fulfilled among us, just as they were handed down to us by those who from the first were eyewitnesses and servants of the word. Therefore, since I myself have carefully investigated everything from the beginning, it seemed good also to me to write an orderly account for you" (Luke 1:1-3, NIV).

Imagine being one of the disciples who worked with Jesus through His ministry and saw Him crucified. Then imagine your inexpressible joy at learning that He was alive! The resurrection of Christ is one of the most powerful attestations to the accuracy of Scripture. Eleven eyewitnesses wrote independently, corroborating one another. For 40 to 60 years they endured persecution for their statements that Christ had returned from the dead, and yet they never denied Him. We fallible humans too easily renounce our faith to save our own lives. No one could ever convince us that cowering Peter or doubting Thomas or any of the other of the apostles of Christ could have maintained a lie for so many years and then been willing to suffer and die for it. Their story *had* to be true! They really *had* seen Jesus alive following His death by crucifixion.

What happened to Jesus' 11 disciples? The Bible and tradition tell us what a few of them experienced. Peter, Andrew, James the son of Alphaeus, Philip, Simon the Zealot, and Bartholomew were crucified. Matthew and James, son of Zebedee, perished by the sword. Tradition claims that Thaddeus was killed by an arrow and Thomas with a spear. Only John, banished to the Isle of Patmos, had a natural death. Stephen, though not one of Jesus' disciples, died from stoning. All of them were willing to suffer and be persecuted or even to die, not because of a lie, but because they had a deep conviction that what they had seen with their own eyes was true. Preaching what they had experienced, they had a reliable message to share, and we can believe it! Thus we have abundant internal evidence that God inspired the New Testament, and that it is therefore completely reliable.

External evidence. But what about external evidence? Do we have anything similar to the Dead Sea scrolls that attests to the accuracy and reliability of the New Testament? The answer is a very positive *yes!* For one thing, the dates of the New Testament documents indicate that they were written within the lifetimes of contemporaries of Christ. People who could remember the things that He had said and did were still alive. Paul composed many of his letters earlier than some of the Gospels. F. F. Bruce, a New Testament scholar, says that the New Testament manuscripts date as much as 200 years earlier than secular historical documents. For example, fewer than a dozen good manuscripts of Caesar's *Gallic Wars* exist, and the oldest of these manuscripts was written approximately 900 years after Caesar's time. The History of Thucydides (c. 460-400 B.C.) is known to us from eight manuscripts, the earliest belonging to about A.D. 900, and a few papyrus scraps, belonging to about the beginning Christian era. The same is true of the History of Herodotus (c. 488-428 B.C.). Yet no classical scholar would listen to an argument that the authenticity of Herodotus or Thucydides is in doubt because the earliest manuscript of their work which are of any use to us are more than 1,300 years later than the originals."[7]

By contrast, many of the New Testament manuscripts are much closer to the events they describe than these secular documents. The earliest manuscript we have is a fragment of a papyrus containing John 18:31-33, 37 dated to around A.D. 130. As noted above, those who wrote the New Testament books lived during the life of Jesus or interviewed those who had walked and talked with Him.

Other external evidence of the reliability of the Bible comes from references and quotations of New Testament books by both friends and enemies of Christianity. The Apostolic Fathers, writing mostly between A.D. 90 and 160, show their familiarity with most of the books of the New Testament. Several of those early nonbiblical writers used Scripture as a reliable and authentic source. Christian writers include Papias (A.D. 130), Clement of Rome (A.D. 95), Ignatius (A.D. 70-110), Polycarp (A.D. 70-156), and Tatian (A.D. 170). They quoted and supported the Bible in their sermons or writings. Their lectionaries and reading lessons used in public church services provide more external evidence. By the middle of the twentieth century scholars had classified more than 1,800 of these reading lessons, containing lectionaries of the Gospels, the book of Acts, and the Epistles. Though they did not appear before the sixth century, the text from which they quote may itself be early and of high quality.[8]

Besides validation by Christian writers, the Bible receives confirmation from such early non-Christian writers as Tacitus, Suetonius, Josephus, Pliny the Younger, the emperor Trajan, the compilers of the Talmud, and many others. For instance, Josephus (A.D. 37-100) spoke of Daniel as a prophet and thus a sixth-century B.C. writer. Josephus referred to Jesus as the brother of James who was martyred. He also confirmed the existence and martyrdom of John the Baptist and gave a brief description of Jesus and His mission.[9] Such reports from early Christian and non-Christian writers complement and confirm the Bible, providing solid external evidence of its truthfulness and reliability.

Reliable Translations
Imagine yourself standing on the Mount of Olives, staring up into the

sky at the disappearing figure of Jesus. His words still ring in your ears: "You will receive power when the Holy Spirit comes on you; and you will be my witnesses in Jerusalem, and in all Judea and Samaria, and to the ends of the earth" (Acts 1:8, NIV). What did He mean by "to the ends of the earth"? As you strain to catch a last glimpse, you remember His command "Therefore go and make disciples of all nations" (Matt. 28:19, NIV). Mark said, quoting Jesus, "Go into all the world and preach the good news to all creation" (Mark 16:15, NIV).

It took the disciples a while to really understand that their mission was to the whole world. Not until Saul became a Christian did the gospel really begin to reach non-Jews. With him, the eternal gospel began to be proclaimed "to those who live on the earth—to every nation, tribe, language and people" (Rev. 14:6, NIV). And the momentum has continued through the ages.

The spread of the gospel required that Christian missionaries teach people in their own languages. Then the new converts wanted to *read* the Bible in their native tongues. By the end of the second century A.D. scholars had translated the New Testament into Syriac, Latin, and Coptic. In A.D. 382 Pope Damascus requested Jerome, the foremost biblical scholar of his day, to make a new translation of the entire Bible into Latin, then the common language of Western Europe. Completed in year 405, it became commonly known as the Vulgate.

In 1380s John Wycliffe produced the first English version. Martin Luther rendered the Bible into German in the early 1500s. They were but two of hundreds to follow. The International Bible Society states that the Bible has now been translated into more than 2,200 languages, reaching some 90 percent of the world's population. Wycliffe Bible Translators has more than 6,000 people working in more than 850 different languages in 50 countries today.[10] Of the languages they are working on, 468 are being translated into for the first time. And Adventist Frontier Missions is currently working on Bible translations (some in picture form for Papua New Guinea) for specific people groups.

A wide variety of translations and versions of the Bible are available in the English language. As you study the Bible, these various versions will give you confidence regarding the accuracy of the many translations. Will the Bible you have in your library be the same as the Bible of 2,000 to 3,000 years ago? Obviously not. It is in English rather than in Greek or Hebrew. But is your Bible relevant for you today? Absolutely! The same Holy Spirit who inspired the Bible speaks through it to your heart, teaching, rebuking, correcting, and training (2 Tim. 3:16), and showing you your need of Jesus.

Arthur S. Maxwell once observed that "the Author's message can always be understood in any language. It never loses its life-giving power. Wherever it goes a river of life flows with it. It has a strange reforming influence, changing people's lives, filling them with courage and hope, and helping them to live aright."[11]

Summary

In this chapter we have shown that there are so few "mistakes" in the Greek and Hebrew manuscripts that they can be regarded as negligible. We have discussed the relevancy of the Bible for us today. While the Bible is not the "same" as it was 2,000 years ago, now being in different languages, the internal and external evidence for both the Old Testament and New Testament scriptures silences the jeers and accusations of the scoffing doubters, proving that the accuracy of translation has preserved the message of its Author. In the next chapter we will examine evidence from archaeology that will provide yet further external evidence regarding the historical validity of the Bible. We conclude by saying that yes, the Bible is truly reliable as God's "owner's handbook" and "love letter" to us, His children.

---

[1] Bernard Ramm, in Josh McDowell, *The New Evidence That Demands a Verdict,* p. 9.

[2] http://www.usc.edu/dept/LAS/wsrp/educational_site/dead_sea_scrolls/discovery.shtml.

[3] In Gerhard F. Hasel, *Understanding the Living Word of God,* Adventist Library of Christian Thought (Mountain View, Calif.: Pacific Press Pub. Assn., 1980), vol. 1, p. 86.

[4] R. Laird Harris, "How Reliable Is the Old Testament Text?" *Can I Trust My Bible?* (Chicago: Moody Press, 1963), p. 124.

[5] *Ibid.,* p. 129.

[6] *Ibid.*

[7] F. F. Bruce, *The New Testament Documents: Are They Reliable?* (Downers Grove, Ill.: InterVarsity Press, 1968), pp. 16, 17.

[8] Paul Little, *Paul Little's What and Why Book* (Minneapolis: World Wide Publications, 1980), p. 190.

[9] *Antiquities of the Jews* 10. 11. 7; 18. 3. 3; 18. 5. 2; 20. 9. 1; see also McDowell, pp. 59, 60.

[10] McDowell, p. 9.

[11] Arthur S. Maxwell, *Your Bible and You* (Washington, D.C.: Review and Herald Pub. Assn., 1959), p. 55.

CHAPTER 5

The Bible and Archaeology

Perhaps you've heard of a period of history during the 1700s known as the Enlightenment. It's also been called the Age of Reason. Some of its more famous philosophers and thinkers were Descartes, Pascal, and Voltaire. It was during this period that science and philosophy began challenging the authority of the Bible and Christianity.

The Enlightenment ultimately gave rise to atheistic Communism, which views religion as harmful to the human race. Karl Marx called religion "the opium of the people." Voltaire boasted that he could utterly destroy the Bible. And during this same period Charles Darwin published his book *On the Origin of Species,* in which he questioned the Creation story.

So-called higher criticism of the Bible also gained popularity during this time. Higher criticism applies to God's Word the same methods used to study any other ancient literature. Higher critics generally deny the inspiration of the Bible, and most also question the historicity of many Bible characters and the stories associated with them.

What does all this have to do with archaeology? About the same time that some thought they had consigned the Bible to the historical trash heap, archaeology began to demonstrate that the Bible is historically accurate.

Biblical Archaeology

The Rosetta Stone was one of the earliest discoveries of what would latter become modern biblical archaeology. The French captain Pierre-François Bouchard discovered this stone in Egypt in 1799 near the town of Rosetta (the modern city of Rashid). It has the same text written on the stone in three different forms of writing. Two of the scripts were from ancient Egypt, the knowledge of which had been lost to the world for more than 1,000 years. The third was Greek, which scholars could read quite well. Thus, by comparing the Greek text with the hieroglyphic and cursive (demotic) texts on the Rosetta Stone, scholars were able to unlock the ancient Egyptian language and read it. This made possible the translation of the writing on thousands of inscriptions found on monuments, tombs, and tablets throughout Egypt.

The next major advance in ancient Near Eastern archaeology was Henry Rawlinson's deciphering of the Behistun Inscription—also in three languages—found in the Kermanshah province of modern Iran. Like the Rosetta Stone, the Behistun Inscription unlocked an ancient type of writing, in this case the Mesopotamian cuneiform scripts that scholars up to that time had been unable to read. The inscription is located 300 feet (100 meters) up the side of a cliff, and it is huge: 45 feet (15 meters) high by 75 feet (25 meters) wide. Its three languages are Old Persian, Elamite, and Babylonian. As a result of Rawlinson's work and that of others, scholars are now able to read the ancient cuneiform writing of the Babylonians.

In 1843 Paul-Émile Botta, a French consul at Mosul, started digging in Khorsabad, which he believed to be the site of biblical Nineveh (it later proved to be the ancient palace of Sargon II). His findings are now at the Louvre in Paris. Several years later Austin Henry Layard visited the true ruins of Nineveh and found amazing treasures. And just a few years afterward, in 1868, the Moabite Stone was uncovered. King Mesha had it inscribed about 850 B.C. It is also now in the Louvre in Paris.

The 1901 discovery of the law code of Hammurabi and the 1964 finding of the Ebla Tablets added to archaeological evidence. Even today archaeologists continue uncovering artifacts that validate the biblical record. Many years ago Nelson Glueck, a Jewish archaeologist, wrote: "It may be stated categorically that no archaeological discovery has ever controverted [refuted] a biblical reference."[1] And his claim is still true. Millar Burrows of Yale observed that "the more archaeologists find, the more the Bible is confirmed. . . . Archaeology has in many cases refuted the views of modern critics. It has shown in a number of instances that these views rest on false assumptions and unreal, artificial schemes of historical development. This is a real contribution and not to be minimized."[2]

Archaeology and Biblical History

The more archaeologists find, the more support the Bible gains. We will look at only a few examples: the Hittites, Sargon, Sennacherib, Nineveh, and Omri. In each instance, archaeological discoveries have either substantiated or enlarged on the biblical record.

The Hittites. For many years some scholars stated categorically that, because known records of ancient history did not mention the Hittites, the Bible simply recorded mythical folklore in its 40-some references to this nation. At best, the scholars said, if the people existed at all, they were merely a small tribe of Palestinians occupying only a village or two. But should we question the historical reliability of the Bible just because the only record of the existence of the Hittites was in the Old Testament?

Again, God's Word proved true. Archaeology has submitted proof after proof of the Hittites' existence. Hieroglyphics on the temple of Karnak and inscriptions on clay tablets found during excavations of the palaces of Assyrian kings have revealed much about this long-lost people. We have found ruins of their ancient cities in Turkey.

We now know that the Hittites began building a powerful empire about 1650 B.C., that they had large fortified cities, and that at one time they ruled a greater part of Asia Minor. Their power was scarcely inferior to that of Assyria or Egypt. They were an Indo-European speaking people whose records date back to about 2000 B.C. The Hittites were the first people to extract iron from ore, enabling them to make weapons and tools of iron.[3] They shared their knowledge with Egypt, and the iron objects of King Tutankhamen's tomb revealed that the critics were wrong about when iron technology became known.[4]

Sargon. Even though the Bible mentions Sargon only once (Isa. 20:1), the history of this king fascinates archaeologists today, and scholars who once claimed that he never existed blush again! He subdued the Hittites and began the demise of their kingdom in 717 B.C. Sargon's palace, excavated in 1843 by Botta in Khorsabad, yielded many treasures. As we noted previously, when Botta first discovered the palace he mistakenly believed that he had found Nineveh. He sent word to France that he had found that ancient city, and its government financed further excavations. They also sent an artist to draw pictures of all the finds. Most of the artifacts were lost because of pirate attacks, but the drawings and one barge's treasures successfully reached France. These constitute ample proof of the majesty of Sargon and his short-lived reign, and they validate the Bible.[5]

Sennacherib. You no doubt remember the story of Sennacherib, the king of Assyria, who challenged King Hezekiah. God sent an angel one night, who slew 185,000 of his men while they slept. So what tragic end came to Sennacherib, and who then took his throne? The Bible says that after he lost those 185,000 men, he broke camp and returned to Nineveh. One day, while he was worshiping in the temple of his god Nisroch, his sons Adrammelech and Sharezer cut him down with the sword, and they escaped to the land of Ararat. And Esarhaddon his son succeeded him as king (2 Kings 19:36, 37). For many years no historical record of Sennacherib existed, and certain critics stated positively that the references to him were pure fiction, along with the story of the angel's miraculous destruction of 185,000 of his men. But an Assyrian record reports that on the twentieth day of the month Tebet, Sennacherib was killed by his son in a revolt. The rebellion continued from the twentieth day of Tebet to the second day of Adar. On the eighteenth of Sivan, Esarhaddon, Sennacherib's son, ascended the throne.

Nineveh. When we hear of Nineveh, we tend to think of Jonah. Jonah 3:3 calls Nineveh "an exceeding great city of three days' journey." Archaeological records show that it was a huge city, completely walled, with 15 great gates. It covered 1,800 acres and was bordered by the Tigris River. Henry A. Layard began excavating the true ruins of Nineveh in 1845 and uncovered Sennacherib's royal palace and the king's royal annals. Layard described the royal palace in these words: "In this magnificent edifice I opened no less than seventy-one halls, chambers, and passages. . . . By a rough calculation, about 9,880 feet, or nearly two miles, of bas-reliefs . . . were uncovered in that part alone.[6]

Omri, king of Israel. The Moabite Stone (found in 1868) tells of Moab's oppression by Omri, king of Israel, and by his son, the infamous Ahab. Again, the biblical narratives find support from archaeology.

Archaeology and Biblical Prophecy

What light does archaeology shed on the prophecies of the Bible? Has anything that would substantiate what God predicted ever been found? We will look at only three prophecies, those regarding Nineveh, Babylon, and Tyre.

Nineveh. At one time the capital of Assyria reached an amazing height of power and glory. It became the center of the ancient Near Eastern world. Yet the Bible predicted the city's demise: "Horsemen charge with bright sword and glittering spear. There is a multitude of slain, a great number of bodies, countless corpses. . . . All who look upon you will . . . say, 'Nineveh is laid waste! Who will bemoan her? Where shall I seek comforters for you?'" (Nahum 3:3-7, NKJV).

How could this be possible for Nineveh, such a powerful city? After all, many other great ancient cities, such as Rome, still continue to exist on their original sites. People first built an important city on a certain spot because that location had specific advantages, such as access to water, food,

45

or routes of travel. And those assets would remain century after century. But God makes biblical prophecy to come to pass.

The combined forces of the Medes and the Babylonians destroyed the city in 612 B.C. They burned the palaces, broke down its temples, and demolished its strong fortifications. All the marvels that Layard found, as described above, were covered with layer upon layer of dirt and sand. The marvelous city had indeed been "laid waste." And, unlike the outcomes of many other ancient cities, people did not return to build upon its ruins.

Babylon. Christian children know the story of Daniel in the lions' den and the fact that he lived in Babylon. Most young people who have attended Adventist schools are probably familiar with Nebuchadnezzar's dream of the great image and Daniel's interpretation that the head of gold represented Babylon. The city's famous Hanging Gardens have been called one of the Seven Wonders of the Ancient World.

Daniel told the proud king, "After you shall arise another kingdom" (Dan. 2:39, NKJV). Isaiah prophesied, "And Babylon, the glory of kingdoms, the beauty of the Chaldeans' pride, will be as when God overthrew Sodom and Gomorrah" (Isa. 13:19, NKJV). He went on to say, "Its houses will be full of howling creatures; there ostriches will dwell, and there satyrs will dance. Hyenas will cry in its towers, and jackals in the pleasant palaces" (Isa. 13:21, 22, RSV). How could this prophecy ever be fulfilled?

Archaeologist Robert Koldewey and his staff spent 14 years of careful work excavating ruined Babylon from 1899 to 1913. Among the most important discoveries they found were:

- Many city gates, of which the Ishtar Gate was the most outstanding.
- The processional street that entered the city at the Ishtar Gate and proceeded directly to the temple of Marduk.
- The gorgeously decorated palace of Nebuchadnezzar, with its banquet hall and throne room.
- The foundation of the Tower of Babel.
- The Hanging Gardens.[7]

How could Babylon ever fall as the Bible prophesied? A famous Adventist archaeologist, Siegfried H. Horn, said of Babylon: "It has been a place of desert animals for centuries, and still gives sanctuary to jackals, hyenas, and owls. Of its former glory nothing has remained except the great name seen on a signpost at the road crossing that leads to the museum and palace ruins."[8]

We will look at only one more prophecy that archaeology has substantiated.

Tyre. We find the first biblical mention of Tyre in Joshua 19:29. The city, however, came into existence much earlier, around the start of the third millennium B.C. You may be familiar with Hiram, king of Tyre, who furnished King Solomon with logs from the famous cedar forests of Lebanon as building materials for his great Temple. Originally Tyre consisted of an island and a land city. King Nebuchadnezzar gained control of the land city, and tried for 13 years to capture the island city of Tyre, but it was so strongly fortified that he failed. Eventually the land city was abandoned; the island city continued to thrive.

Later Alexander the Great succeeded in conquering the island city by dumping the ruins of the coastal city into the sea, building a causeway connecting land and island, and then rolling his battering rams to the walls of the city that was no longer an island. This "queen city of the sea" still exists in a very small way today. Fisherman spread their nets over the ruins of the ancient land city, in fulfillment of another biblical prophecy. Ezekiel said that Tyre's walls would be destroyed, its towers pulled down, and its rubble scraped away, making it a "bare rock. Out in the sea she will become a place to spread fishnets. . . . She will become plunder for the nations, and her settlements on the mainland will be ravaged by the sword. Then they will know that I am the Lord" (Eze. 26:4-6, NIV). Verses 12-14 predict exactly what happened: "They will . . . demolish your fine houses and throw your stones, timber and rubble into the sea. . . . I will make you a bare rock, and you will become a place to spread fishnets. You will never be rebuilt, for I the Lord have spoken, declares the Sovereign Lord" (NIV). Both historical records and the mute debris of the once-proud city attest to the accuracy of the prediction.

In a statement that is still true today even decades after he made it, Sir Frederic Kenyon said:

"To my mind, the true and valuable thing to say about archaeology is, not that it proves the Bible, but that it illustrates the Bible. The contribution of archaeology to Bible study has been to widen and deepen our knowledge of the background of the Bible narrative, and especially of the Old Testament. . . . The trend of all this increased knowledge has been to confirm the authority of the books of the Old Testament while it illuminates their interpretation. Destructive criticism is thrown on the defensive; and the plain man may read his Bible confident that, for anything that modern research has to say, the Word of our God shall stand forever."[9]

Bible Stories Enriched Through Archaeology

Archaeology serves as testimony to the accuracy of the Bible's history and its prophecies. It also enhances the stories of the Bible, and adds color to our understanding of the times in which those events happened. We will look at Abraham, Moses, and the Canaanite culture.

Abraham. The discovery of the law code of Hammurabi in 1901 in Shushan and an excavation in Nuzi have shown that some of the practices of the patriarchs mentioned in the Bible conform accurately to the culture of their times. One example is Sarah giving her slave girl to Abraham as a surrogate wife (Gen. 16:1-3). Another is Esau's selling his birthright for food (Gen. 25:33). A third is Laban giving each of his daughters, Leah and Rachel, a handmaid at the time of their marriage (Gen. 29:24, 29). All were common practices in the ancient Near East, as elucidated in the Hammurabi code. The fascinating study of archaeology can help us understand much more about the customs of those living during Bible times.

Moses. When we read that Moses turned his back on the treasures of Egypt, most of us have little appreciation of what that meant. What had he declined? In 1922 Howard Carter discovered the tomb of Tutankhamen, who lived in the fourteenth century B.C. The Cairo Museum displays more than 1,700 objects found in Tutankhamen's tomb. They include the king's mask of pure gold and many other precious ornaments. This one tomb alone had multimillion dollars' worth of dazzling treasures. Yet Moses abandoned those kinds of things because he saw "Him who is invisible" (Heb. 11:27, NKJV). Moses acted "by faith." While none of us will ever have to discard the enormous wealth that Moses did, would we be strong enough to follow his example of faith?

Canaanite culture. According to the Bible, the Canaanites had a very corrupt religion. Extrabiblical sources shed a great deal of light on their religious practices. The archaeological discovery of Ras Shamra in 1929 contained written cuneiform documents among the ruins of a temple school. They provide us with an actual record of the Canaanite religion. Siegfried Horn said that "these texts, being mythological in nature, tell us what the Canaanites believed about their gods, of which the most famous was *El,* called 'the father of years,' and *Baal,* the god of fertility, with his ferocious and immoral sister *Anath,* and *Asherah,* a female goddess, often mentioned in the Old Testament. . . . We learn that the Canaanites considered their gods to be immoral beings, who also delighted in bloodshed and cruelty. Since the religion of these people must reflect their own morality, and the ideas about their gods must mirror their own ethics, we can understand that the degradation of the Canaanites at the time of these texts—in the middle of the second millennium B.C.—must have reached such a low point that God could not allow His people to mingle with these immoral idolaters."[10]

Archaeology Aids in Better Translation

Archaeology has also enabled better Bible translations. For example, the word *chamman* appears eight times in the Old Testament, and the King James Version rendered it as "image" seven times and "idol" once (Lev. 26:30; 2 Chron. 14:5; 34:4, 7; Isa. 17:8; 27:9; Eze. 6:4, 6). The American Standard Version used "sun-image" for it. An archaeological excavation in Palmyra, Syria, discovered an incense altar that had the word *chamman* inscribed on it. Thus we know that the word ought to be translated "incense altar." This shows how archaeological discoveries can help Bible translators to be more accurate, even though no basic idea is in any way affected.[11]

Summary

We have seen that archaeological finds help refute the criticism of the Bible that began in the Age of Enlightenment and that continues even today. Archaeology supports biblical history, confirms Bible prophecy, enlightens biblical stories, and aids in creating more accurate translations. Sir Frederic Kenyon, a former director of the British Museum, wrote that "it is therefore legitimate to say that, in respect of that part of the Old Testament against which the disintegrating criticism of the last half of the nineteenth century was chiefly directed, the evidence of archaeology has been to reestablish its authority and likewise to augment its value by rendering it more intelligible through a fuller knowledge of its background and setting. Archaeology has not yet said its last word; but the results already achieved confirm what faith would suggest, that the Bible can do nothing but gain from an increase in knowledge."[12]

Archaeology, as external evidence, strengthens our faith in the Bible and in its Author, who loved us too much to leave us wondering whether or not we had a safe and reliable "owner's manual." Truly we can absolutely trust our awesome God's love letter to us!

---

[1] Nelson Glueck, *Rivers in the Desert* (New York: Farrar, Straus and Cudahy, 1959), p. 31.

[2] Millar Burrows, *What Mean These Stones?* (New York: Meridian Books, 1956), p. 29.

[3] http://home.cfl.rr.com/crossland/AncientCivilizations/Middle_East_Civilizations/Hittites/hittites.html.

[4] Siegfried Horn, *The Spade Confirms the Book* (Washington, D.C.: Review and Herald Pub. Assn., 1957), p. 121.

[5] http://en.wikipedia.org/wiki/Sargon_of_Akkad; http://en.wikipedia.org/wiki/713_BC.

[6] Frank C. Thompson, ed., *Thompson Chain-Reference Bible* (Grand Rapids: Zondervan Bible Pub., 1983) p. 1681.

[7] *Ibid.*, p. 1636.

[8] Horn, p. 51.

[9] Sir Frederic Kenyon, *Journal of Transactions of the Victoria Institute* (London: 1941), pp. 83–92.

[10] Horn, p. 256.

[11] T. H. Jemison, *Christian Beliefs*, p. 36.

[12] Sir Frederic Kenyon, *The Bible and Archaelogy* (New York: Harper & Brothers, 1940), p. 279.

CHAPTER 6

The Bible and Science

"There is no way science and the Bible can both be true," a friend once assured me. "The more I study, the more archaic the Bible seems."

That was years ago, and I did not know how to reply. Today I know that significant evidence in science confirms the reliability of the Bible. In an article entitled "A Scientist Faces a Crisis," James C. Hefley tells the experience of Dr. Howard A. Kelly. Kelly, a surgeon and professor of surgery at Johns Hopkins University during the 1930s, came to a personal crisis over a method of interpreting the Bible called "higher criticism." Higher critics claim that the Bible is a purely human book, that its prophecies were written after the events that they predicted had come to pass, and that its miracle stories are mere Hebrew folklore.[1]

Kelly decided to discover from the Bible what it had to say about itself. He learned that from Genesis to Revelation the Bible claims to be God's personal message to His children. So he accepted the Bible as the "textbook" of the Christian faith, just as he did medical literature writings as his textbooks in medicine. Finally, he submitted to Jesus' summons to obedience: "If anyone chooses to do God's will, he will find out whether my teaching comes from God or whether I speak on my own" (John 7:17, NIV). From his study he concluded that the Bible must be accepted by faith as the inspired Word of God, different from any human book. Dr. Kelly came to be recognized both for his personal commitment to Scripture and as a towering witness in the scientific community. When he faced a crisis of belief, he examined his faith more closely and came out stronger than ever before.[2]

More than seven decades have passed since Dr. Kelly's discovery about the reliability of the Bible. Since then the scientific method has become almost the god of our age. Can we still accept the Bible and its foundational role in our lives not only spiritually but also intellectually? Fortunately, recent numerous scientific discoveries show that contradictions between Scripture and science are frequently the result of speculation. When we cannot harmonize science with Scripture, it is because we have "an imperfect comprehension of either science or revelation . . . ; but rightly understood, they are in perfect harmony."[3] In this chapter we will examine several important biblical passages in light of modern scientific discoveries that show that the Bible and science are compatible.

Archaeological Evidence of a Global Flood

Many people today question the reality of a worldwide flood. It means that they question the truthfulness of the Bible. However, various intellectual fields such as archaeology provide significant evidence in support of a global flood. For example, an ancient Mesopotamian story discovered by archaeologists shows numerous similarities with the Bible's flood narrative, suggesting a lingering memory of an ancient event. Notice the following points:

- The story tells of someone who survived a massive flood.
- The flood was a divine judgment against humanity.
- The deity commanded the story's hero to build a ship and forsake his possessions in order to save his life.
- The deity ordered him to bring animals and his family into the ship.
- The deity gave the measurements of the ship.
- The hero obeyed and received a message for his fellow citizens.
- The deity instructed the hero to enter the ship.
- A terrifying storm and rain caused the flood.
- All human beings not in the ship perished.
- The ship landed on a mountain after the waters had receded.
- The hero sent birds out to gather evidence concerning the drying up of the earth.
- After disembarkation the hero offered a sacrifice.
- The deity accepted the sacrifice.[4]

And the Mesopotamian narrative is just one of many ancient flood stories. According to Russell Chandler, author of the book *Doomsday: The End of the World—A View Through Time,* there are "about two hundred versions of the Flood story told and retold down through the ages. . . . Accounts have been found in every region and among nearly all the nations and tribes of the world. Although scholars . . . differ over the explanation, the simplest is that there was once such a flood."[5]

Geological Evidence of a Global Flood

Some physical evidence exists to show that a worldwide flood could have occurred in the past.

- The great abundance and widespread distribution of marine deposits on the continents is consistent with the Genesis flood story.
- The widespread sedimentary depots with land fossils on the continents is evidence of some kind of catastrophic activity.
- "The burial of vast numbers of animals quickly and without noticeable decay" "constitutes . . . remarkable evidence of rapid water movement and flooding."[6]
- The extensive coal beds, the end product of organic matter transformed by tremendous pressure, attests to the massive amounts of once-living things that got buried. One of the most probable causes of such coal deposits is a global flood.[7]

Astronomy

The Bible writers often mention the beauty and majesty of the starry heavens with a sense of awe. The psalmist said, "The heavens declare the glory of God" (Ps. 19:1). Elsewhere he declared that "the host of heaven cannot be numbered" (Jer. 33:22).

The ancients, who observed the universe with just the naked eye, tried to count the stars, and the numbers they came up with varied. Ptolemeus cataloged 1,056 stars, Tycho Brahe was able to list only 777, while Kepler said there were 1,005. Before the invention of the telescope in the seventeenth century, some believed that the universe had 5,119 stars. We now know that often what they thought were individual stars were actually whole galaxies or clusters of stars!

The Palomar Mountain telescope has a 200-inch reflector lens that has revealed hundreds of billions of stars. "The huge 200-inch Hale reflector on Palomar Mountain—the world's largest optical telescope—can see as many as a million galaxies inside the bowl of the Big Dipper alone."[8] Orbiting telescopes such as the Hubble Space Telescope as well as X-ray and radio telescopes have detected even more stars.

No one can say for sure how many stars actually exist, but God can. In fact, the Bible says that He has even named each one of them. "He determines the number of the stars and calls them each by name" (Ps. 147:4, NIV). Just as Adam named the animals in accordance with their distinctive characteristics (Gen. 2:19, 20), so God has named the stars.

Geophysics

We know from scientific evidence that the earth is round. However, for centuries critics of the Bible said that its authors portrayed the world as flat and stationary: an earth with four corners, perhaps resting on giant pillars, with the sun, moon, and stars orbiting it daily along the surface of a great celestial sphere. Such a cosmology may have been the concept of the medieval church, strongly influenced by Greek and Roman philosophy, but the Bible teaches no such thing. In fact, the Scriptures were far in advance of modern science in their assertion of the size, shape, support, and rotation of the earth. What does the Bible say about the shape of the world?

"It is He who sits above the *circle* of the earth" (Isa. 40:22, NKJV). How did the Bible writer know this? Speaking of divine wisdom, Scripture says, "I was there when he set the heavens in place, when he marked out the horizon on the face of the deep" (Prov. 8:27, NIV). The word "horizon" in this verse and the word "circle" in Isaiah 40:22 "are both translations of the same Hebrew *chuwg,* an excellent rendering of which is 'circle.' It could well be used also for 'sphere,' since there seems to have been no other ancient Hebrew word with this explicit meaning (a sphere is simply the figure formed by a circle turning about its diameter)."[9]

Many other Bible verses show that the Bible was ahead of science. The following are two examples:

"The heavens shall pass away with a great noise, and the elements shall melt with fervent heat" (2 Peter 3:10). Only in recent years have scientists learned that global destruction is possible through nuclear fission, though God may indeed use some other method when He brings earth's history to its fiery end.

"He spreads out the northern skies over empty space; he suspends the earth over nothing" (Job 26:7, NIV). Not until A.D. 1530 did Copernicus discover that the earth was suspended in space. Actually the Hebrew word used is rather emphatic. It means "nothing whatever." The earth is neither resting on pillars nor suspended from some heavenly ceiling. Instead, the force of gravity maintains it in an orbit about the sun.

Public Health

The Bible reveals much regarding public health. Bible students can find information about sanitation, nutrition, and public health that were far ahead of scientific discoveries. For example, the Bible says, "The life of every creature is its blood" (Lev. 17:14, NIV), a fact proven in A.D. 1615 when William Harvey discovered the function of blood in the human body.

God gave many commandments that have a physical health emphasis. Some examples are the laws found in Leviticus 11 and Deuteronomy 14. They prohibited the eating of camels, hares, swine, dogs, cats, weasels, mice, and lizards. Medical science has proved that abstaining from consuming the flesh of such animals will limit the incidence of numerous diseases.[10] Note, for example, what scientists have discovered about pork. We know that it has the highest fat content of all meat. A high-fat diet can clog the arteries and make a person prone to a heart attack. And heart disease is the leading cause of death in developed countries.

In addition to the fat problem, Dr. J. B. McNaught, who examined pork specimens in the San Francisco meat markets, found that one out of four pig carcasses had living trichina larvae in it.[11] Symptoms from such larval invasions include bleeding and pain in the eyes, muscle soreness, itchy skin, and bleeding under the nails and in the lungs. Such symptoms can appear between the fourth and the eighth week after eating infected pork products. Most symptoms disappear by about the third month, although muscle pain and tiredness may persist for months.

The Bible truly is far ahead of science in advising us not to eat pork because of its negative impact on health.

Scripture gives explicit guidelines regarding clean and unclean fish. "Of all the creatures living in the waters . . . you may eat any that have fins and scales. But all . . . that do not have fins and scales . . . you are to detest" (Lev. 11:9, 10, NIV). Do we have any scientific evidence that "clean" fish are better than "unclean" fish?

During World War II American naval aviators shot down over the ocean had no choice but to survive on whatever seafood they could catch. However, they often became very ill. Consequently, the U.S. government hired a marine biologist, Bruce Halsted, to research what kinds of fish downed pilots could eat safely. Halsted developed a thick manual, showing pictures of the fish that were safe to eat and those that were not. He also said, "If you lose this manual, remember one thing: if it has fins and scales, you can eat it. If it doesn't have fins and scales—such as crab, lobster, shrimp, oysters, clams—don't eat it, because they have a high level of toxicity."[12] That twentieth-century marine biologist echoed the Word of God.

Mental Health

Another example of the Bible stating facts long before science discovered them occurs in Proverbs 17:22: "A cheerful heart is good medicine,

55

but a crushed spirit dries up the bones" (NIV). Is it really true that a cheerful heart is beneficial to our health?

The late Norman Cousins, who authored the book *Anatomy of an Illness as Perceived by the Patient,* edited the *Saturday Review* for 30 years and served as adjunct professor of psychiatry and biobehavioral science at the University of California at Los Angeles. In his book he related his personal experience with a serious inflammatory disease. The skin on his hands became thick, tight, and shiny. He had difficulty moving his fingers and his limbs, and turning over in bed was hard. He also had lumps over all of his body. His mouth was almost locked shut.

Doctors prescribed the maximum dosage of painkilling and sedative drugs, as a result of which Cousins developed hives all over his body. His skin felt as if millions of red ants were biting his skin. One day Cousins told his doctor, "I am really tired of all these medications and their side effects. I want to quit and try to make myself happy." So he called Allen Funt, the producer of the popular TV program *Candid Camera,* and asked him to send some amusing movies and a projector. To his surprise, Cousins discovered that 10 minutes of genuine belly laughter relieved the pain enough for him to be able to sleep at least two hours.

At the end of eight days Cousins was able to move his thumbs without pain. Then the lumps on his neck and back began to shrink. Eventually he recovered enough to return to his full-time job as editor of the *Saturday Review.* Year by year his mobility improved until he could play tennis and golf, ride a horse, hold a camera with a steady hand, and play the piano.[13]

Laughter exercises the lungs and stimulates the circulatory system, thus increasing the amount of oxygen taken into the lungs. In many ways laughter is like an internal jogger—heart rate, breathing, and circulation will speed up after good and hearty laughter, and subsequently the pulse rate and blood pressure will decrease and the skeletal muscles may then become relaxed.[14] In some cases real laughter can relieve pain more effectively than morphine. Truly laughter is a powerful medicine!

Science proves not only the blessing of having a merry heart, but also the opposite. Solomon said that "a crushed spirit dries up the bones" (Prov. 17:22, NIV). The twentieth-century lifestyle studies by Drs. Nedra Belloc and Lester Breslow from the Department of Public Health, Berkeley, California, affirm that longevity has a close connection with a person's happy disposition. The study involved 6,928 adult residents of Alameda County, and the results showed that those who were generally unhappy had a much higher death rate than those who were generally very happy.[15]

Harvard University students participated in an experiment. They completed a comprehensive personality test that measured their tolerance, confidence, and self-esteem. The researchers took a blood sample, isolated "natural killer" cells, and exposed them to cancer cells. After four hours the natural killer cells from students who had a positive attitude destroyed more cancer cells than any other personality group. On the other hand, the natural killer cells from students who ranked high on the depression scale and were inclined to withdrawal and maladjustment were the least active in destroying cancer cells.[16] The study demonstrates the truth of Proverbs 3:7, 8, which says, "Fear the Lord and shun evil. This will bring health to your body and nourishment to your bones" (NIV).

Modern science has demonstrated that the bone marrow produces immune cells. How interesting that the Bible uses the analogy of the bones as a source of health! What the Bible said long ago really is correct.

During recent years "evidence has accumulated that psychology can indeed affect biology. Studies have found, for example, that people who suffer from depression are at higher risk for heart disease and other illnesses. Other research has shown that wounds take longer to heal in women who care for patients with Alzheimer's disease than in other women not similarly stressed. And people under stress have been found to be more susceptible to colds and flu, and to have more severe symptoms after they fall ill."[17]

A recent study from the University of Wisconsin indicates that "the activation of brain regions associated with negative emotions appears to weaken people's immune response to a flu vaccine."[18]

Summary

We can use the Bible's scientific principles to lead people to trust the Bible, because God's "owners' manual" and scientific love letter to His beloved children is superior to science.

---

[1] In *Practical Christianity,* ed. LaVonne Neff et al. (Wheaton, Ill.: Tyndale House Publishers, Inc., 1987), p. 100.

[2] *Ibid.,* pp. 100, 101.

[3] Ellen G. White, *Patriarchs and Prophets* (Mountain View, Calif.: Pacif Press Pub. Assn., 1890), p. 114.

[4] *The Seventh-day Adventist Bible Commentary,* vol. 1, p. 116.

[5] Russell Chandler, *Doomsday: The End of the World—A View Through Time* (Ann Arbor, Mich.: Servant Publications, 1993), p. 36.

[6] Harold G. Coffin, *Creation—Accident or Design?* (Washington, D.C.: Review and Herald Pub. Assn., 1969), p. 69.

[7] *Ibid.,* p. 75.

[8] *National Geographic,* May 1974, p. 592.

[9] Henry M. Morris, *The Biblical Basis for Modern Science* (Green Forest, Ark.: Master Books, Inc., 2002), p. 227.

[10] Harvey Rosenstock and Donald G. Dawe, "Moses, the Father of Preventive Medicine," *Minnesota Medicine* 47 (February 1964): 171.

[11] Mark Finley, *Discoveries in Prophecy* (Fallbrook, Calif.: Hart Research Center, 1995), p. 8.

[12] *Ibid.,* p. 9.

[13] Norman Cousins, *Anatomy of an Illness as Perceived by the Patient* (New York: W. W. Norton & Company, Inc., 1979), pp. 27-43.

[14] http://www.hhp.ufl.edu/faculty/pbird/keepingfit/ARTICLE/LAF.HTM.

[15] L. F. Berkman and S. L. Syme, "Social Networks, Host Resistance, and Mortality: A Nine-Year Follow-up Study of Almeida County Residents," *American Journal of Epidemiology* 109, no. 2 (February 1979): 186-204.

[16] J. K. Kiecolt-Glaser, W. Garner, C. E. Speicher, G. Penn, and R. Vlaser, "Psychosocial Modifiers of Immunocompetence in Medical Students," *Psychosomatic Medicine* 46 (1984): 7-14.

[17] Erica Goode, "Power of Positive Thinking May Have a Health Benefit, Study Says," New York *Times,* Sept. 2, 2003.

[18] *Ibid.*

CHAPTER 7

The Bible Changes
Our Lives

End of the Spear, a recent movie based on the book by the same title, chronicles the amazing power of the gospel of Jesus Christ to transform Stone Age savages into peaceful, loving people.

Five Ecuadorian natives from the Waodani tribe brutally murdered Steve Saint's father, Nate Saint, and four other missionaries on January 8, 1956. Yet today Steve and his father's killer travel around the world together, powerfully proclaiming the story of the transforming grace found in the Word of God.

How did these Indians learn about God's grace? In his book Steve tells how his aunt Rachel (his murdered father's sister) chose to remain living with the Ecuadorian tribe at their invitation, while she painstakingly translated the Bible into their dialect. She then taught a few of them to read, all the while telling them stories of Jesus and the principles of peace found in the Bible. Slowly many of these people began to "walk the Jesus way."

Clarence W. Hall, a war correspondent on Okinawa, experienced meeting a strange and most inspiring community when he arrived in Shimabuku early in 1945. He and his group were welcomed as "fellow Christians." He tells his story in the following words:

"Guided by the two old men—Mojun Nakamura the mayor and Shosei Kina the schoolmaster—we cautiously toured the compound. We'd seen other Okinawan villages uniformily down-at-the-heels and despairing; by contrast, this one shone like a diamond in a dung heap. Proudly the two old men showed us their spotless homes, their terraced fields, fertile and neat, their storehouses and granaries, their prized sugar mill." What had happened?

"Thirty years before, an American missionary on his way to Japan had paused at Shimabuku. He'd stayed only long enough to make a pair of converts (these same two men), teach them a couple of hymns, leave them

59

a Japanese translation of the Bible and exhort them to live by it. They'd had no contact with any Christian since. Yet . . . guided by the Bible, they had managed to create a Christian democracy at its purest. . . .

"The two converts had found not only an inspiring 'Person' on whom to pattern a life, but sound precepts on which to base their society.

"They'd adopted the Ten Commandments as Shimabuku's legal code; the Sermon on the Mount as their guide to social conduct. In Kina's school the Bible was the chief literature; it was read daily by all students, and major passages were memorized. In Nakamura's village government the precepts of the Bible were law. Nurtured on this Book, a whole generation of Shimabukans had drawn from it their ideas of human dignity and of the rights and responsibilities of citizenship.

"The result was plain to see. Shimabuku for years had no jail, no brothel, no drunkenness, no divorce; there was a high level of health and happiness."[1]

The lives of some 1,000 Shimabukans show that the Bible has the ability to change people's lives. Like the Shimabukans, thousands of people's lives have been transformed as the result of reading their Bibles. In centuries past millions renounced their idolatry, gave up their pagan sacrifices and the rites of such gods, and forsook their temples. Many cannibalistic communities have abandoned their cruel practices and become loving ones.

The Bible is the most influential book in the world. Having converted millions of people, transformed whole countries, and changed the course of civilization, it is the tool that the Spirit uses to transform us (Eph. 1:17). A living power, sharper than any two-edged sword (Heb. 4:12), it is capable of making its way into any human heart that is open to God's message.

The Bible the Agent of Change

We know we are all sinners. Paul wrote, "None is righteous, no, not one. . . . No one seeks for God. All have turned aside, together they have gone wrong; no one does good, not even one" (Rom. 3:10-12, RSV). Isaiah, commenting on the human condition, observed, "Your hands are defiled with blood and your fingers with iniquity; your lips have spoken lies, your tongue mutters wickedness" (Isa. 59:3, RSV). No wonder the Bible asks, "Can the Ethiopian change his skin or its leopard his spots? Neither can you do good who are accustomed to doing evil" (Jer. 13:23, NIV). We can't transform our sinful nature.

However, there's good news! Anybody who begins to read Scripture will find Jesus to be the way, the truth, and the life (John 14:6). Only He has the ability to alter people's hearts. The Bible reveals His life and death, the divine plan of salvation, and His desire to make us over. Just as seeds grow and produce fruit, so also the Word of God, once it penetrates human hearts, will produce the fruits of repentance and change.

The Word of God has life-giving power in it. Luke 8:11 tells us that "the seed is the word." Ellen White explains that "the word of God is the seed. Every seed has in itself a germinating principle. . . . So there is life in God's Word. . . . In every command and in every promise of the Word of God is the power, the very life of God, by which the command may be fulfilled and the promise realized."[2] The author of Hebrews speaks of the power of Jesus' word: He is "the radiance of God's glory and the exact representation of his being, sustaining all things by *his powerful word*" (Heb. 1:3, NIV). The word "powerful" comes from Greek word *dunamis,* from which we get our word "dynamite." The Word of God has explosive power to change people's lives for the better!

Reading Scripture helps us to know Jesus. Because the Bible is truth and has great power, the more we read of it the more we know Him, become convicted of our sins, and find strength to overcome them. Thus we become changed, as were the Waodani of Ecuador and the Shimabuku of Okinawa.

The Bible: Source of Faith

Consider the following biblical passages:

- Romans 1:17: "The just shall live by *faith.*"
- Ephesians 2:8: "For by *grace* are ye saved through *faith.*"
- Romans 7:24, 25: "Who will rescue [save] me from this body of death? Thanks be to God—through Jesus Christ our Lord!" (NIV).

In light of such texts, how would you say we are saved? By faith? By grace? By Jesus? It is not a hypothetical question, nor is it an unsolvable dilemma. Rather it is somewhat like a circle that goes round and round. You will find people who have entered the circle at different points. Peter, for example, finally and fully entered into salvation when he experienced Jesus' marvelous forgiving grace.

The apostle Paul's life altered when a vision of Jesus struck him down. He then became the primary champion of the gospel of salvation through faith in Jesus and His grace—a grace powerful enough to radically change his whole way of life.

As he sat alone, blind, for three days in Damascus, Paul's keen mind, actuated by the Holy Spirit, revisited all the Scriptures he had long ago memorized. Overwhelmed by the testimony regarding Jesus, he opened his heart and accepted Him as his own Savior, in whom he now had faith. After the restoration of his sight, he left Damascus and spent several years in Arabia, searching the Scriptures. The Bible, God's Word, became the solid foundation of his faith.

"Faith comes from hearing the message, and the message is heard through the word of Christ" (Rom. 10:17, NIV). We could describe Paul's experience, as well as yours and mine, something like this circle:

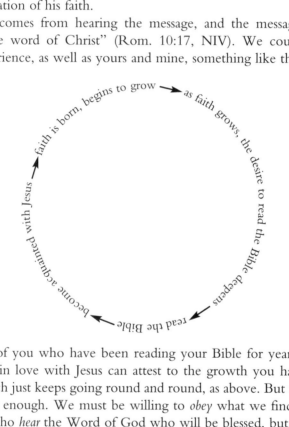

Those of you who have been reading your Bible for years and who have fallen in love with Jesus can attest to the growth you have experienced, which just keeps going round and round, as above. But reading the Bible is not enough. We must be willing to *obey* what we find in it. It is not those who *hear* the Word of God who will be blessed, but those who *obey* the Word of God (James 1:22). Approaching the Bible without any prejudice, we need to read Scripture with the desire to apply it to our lives and adjust our lives according to God's will. Always we should open the Bible with the prayer "Open my eyes that I may see wonderful things in Your law." If we come to the Bible with humility and the desire to do His will, He will guide us, and we will continually progress in our spiritual journey. The spirit of humility and a willingness to change will build our faith in what we learn from our reading and from listening to the Holy

Spirit. Reading the Bible with a spirit of humility and being willing to be led by the Holy Spirit's promptings will forever transform our lives.

The Principles of Life

Isaiah wrote, "To the law and to the testimony: if they speak not according to this word, it is because there is no light in them" (Isa. 8:20). We then see why we need to present the Word of God, for without it there is no light.

The Bible, being inspired or God-breathed (2 Tim. 3:16), is no ordinary book. Although it has existed for nearly 2,000 years, it contains specific and detailed information that will guide us in the situations we encounter from day to day. The pen of inspiration says, "In the Bible every vital principle is declared, every duty made plain, every obligation made evident."[3] No matter what situation we face, we can always find scriptural guidance. Help is available as we study biblical biographies, the life and teachings of Jesus, and specific doctrinal teachings.

True, the Bible does not give instruction on every problem. At times God's will seems unclear. Then we must search for biblical *principles,* asking for guidance by the indwelling of the Holy Spirit. We can learn to walk in the Spirit and be sensitive to God by saturating our minds with Scripture. The Bible compares itself to a lamp (Ps. 119:105), to food (Matt. 4:4), to a hammer and to fire (Jer. 23:29), to honey (Ps. 119:103), and to a sword (Eph. 6:17). All of these symbolize things that transform something else, indicating how Scripture—if we let it—will guide us in reaching Spirit-guided decisions.

The Bible reveals the will of a loving, living God who has a plan for each of us. Scripture can educate our ethics and tell us what He expects. It may not tell us the exact answer to a question we might have, but it reveals to us the kind of person we should be. Once we have become more like that person, our transformed minds will be able to make the decisions and come to the conclusions that will answer our many questions. A Spirit-guided character will have Spirit-guided judgment and discernment. And as we follow God's divine plan for us, life-changing happiness results.

The Power of Revival

How often we hear people say, "We need to have a revival in our church!" In fact, inspiration tells us: "Revival of true godliness among us is the greatest and most urgent of all our needs. To seek this should be our first work."[4] What is revival? J. J. Packer defines it as "a work of God by

His Spirit through His Word bringing the spiritually dead to living faith in Christ and renewing the inner life of Christians who have grown slack and sleepy." He further adds, "Revival thus animates or reanimates churches and Christian groups to make a spiritual and moral impact on communities. It comprises an initial reviving, followed by a maintained state of revivedness."[5]

The marks of genuine revival are: (1) a sense of the presence of God and the truth of the gospel; (2) an awareness of sin that leads to repentance; (3) a heartfelt embrace of the glorified, loving, pardoning Christ; (4) an intensifying and speeding up of the work of grace; (5) many conversions; (6) and community involvement in the revival.[6]

While we recognize that revival cannot possibly happen without the Holy Spirit, we also know that the Holy Spirit is the author of the Bible (2 Peter 1:21). So the Holy Spirit uses the Bible to bring revival, and the study of the Bible prepares the way for the Holy Spirit. It works both ways—another circular effect. Jesus said: "The words that I speak unto you, they are spirit, and they are life" (John 6:63). Studying the Bible helps us to see that all genuine revivals are related to an increased study of the Word of God.

Pentecost was the beginning of genuine Christian revival, with 3,000 people baptized in one day. If we study Peter's sermon in Acts carefully, we can see that he focused on Scripture. Of the 26 verses in Peter's discourse (Acts 2:14-36, 38-40), 11 quote directly from the Old Testament, and 12 devote themselves to an explanation of those Old Testament passages. The remaining three verses are direct appeals (verses 38-40). Thus we see that Peter's sermon was essentially a Bible study.

Revival is not only the result of Bible study—it is also related to the preaching of the Word of God. Acts 10:44 says: "While Peter was still speaking these words, the Holy Spirit fell upon all those who heard the word" (NKJV). Bible study leads to revival, and revival will enhance further Bible study. No wonder Ellen White declares: "Let us give more time to the study of the Bible. We do not understand the word as we should. . . . When we as a people understand what this book [Revelation] means to us, there will be seen among us a great revival."[7]

The Power of Reformation

What happens to churches that have experienced great revival? In many cases God's work in energizing His church has been wasted because we have pursued revival without having reformation. "Revival is the starting line, not the finish line. After revival begins, the real work starts. Revival brings power; reformation transforms that power into lasting change. We need to go beyond the inspiration of the moment, beyond the event mentality, beyond conventional thinking to find a process that leads to lasting change."[8]

The Bible gives a number of examples of revivals followed by a genuine reformation. King Jehoshaphat sent preachers who used "the book of the law" as they went throughout all the cities of Judah (2 Chron. 17:9). The Written Word—Scripture—served as the basis of this revival, which reformation then accompanied.

Elisha carried Elijah's revival into a reformation in Israel.

Ezra and Nehemiah worked together to bring about a revival, resulting in reformation so far-reaching that people sent away foreign wives and their children and stopped the buying and selling that had been going on during the Sabbath hours (Ezra 10:3; Neh. 8:1, 2; 13:15-21).

Scripture clearly describes the changed attitudes and lives that accompany true revival. The Spirit of God fits those involved to "run the race" described in Scripture (1 Cor. 9:24-27; Heb. 12:1, 2). The Bible becomes the guideline of their lives. Growing spiritual maturity leads to an increased power of judgment (1 Cor. 2:15, 16). Obedience to the will of God as taught in the Bible expresses itself in joy. Those who experience revival and reformation will not ignore scriptural teaching. The goal envisioned by the prophet Jeremiah is that God's law will be written on the heart, so that it not only permeates our thinking but also becomes our very life and breath (Jer. 31:33, 34).

Summary

We have learned that reading the Bible with a teachable heart will change our lives. Personal study of Scripture will bring personal revival and transformation, and public proclamation of Scripture will bring corporate change. Divine energy and power fill the Bible. Its words live because it is the Word of the living God. And Scripture is not merely the living Word, but is life-giving as well. The life of God Himself is imparted to the one who believes and appropriates the living Word.

Scripture clearly describes the changes in attitude and life that happen to those who experience true revival. Such changes enable them to "run the race" described in Scripture. The Bible becomes the guideline of their lives. With growing maturity comes increased power of judgment (1 Cor. 2:15). Obedience to the will of God as expressed in the Bible becomes their joy. Those who experience revival and reformation allow God to write His law on their hearts. It becomes their very life and breath.

———————

[1] http://www.crossroad.to/Victory/testimonies/Japan.htm.

[2] E. G. White, *Christ's Object Lessons,* p. 38.

[3] Ellen G. White, *Fundamental of Christian Education* (Nashville: Southern Pub. Assn., 1923), p. 187.

[4] White, *Selected Messages,* book 1, p. 121.

[5] In Bill Hull, *Revival That Reforms* (Grand Rapids: Fleming H. Revell, 1998), p. 29.

[6] *Ibid.*

[7] Ellen G. White, *Testimonies to Ministers* (Mountain View, Calif.: Pacific Press Pub. Assn., 1923), p. 113.

[8] Hull, p. 11.

CHAPTER 8

The Bible Gives Us Hope

A pediatrician urged a couple to have an abortion, because the wife had contracted chicken pox during the first trimester of the pregnancy of their third child. The doctor said the baby might be born with missing limbs, half a face, or at least some form of neurological damage.

Despite the seemingly hopeless situation, the parents refused to consider abortion. "At one point I got a mental picture of microscopic angels holding the chicken pox virus away from our baby," the father said. After the child's birth, the parents named him Samuel Victor because their prayers were "heard of the Lord," who gave the infant "victory" over the chicken pox virus. At the time of this writing, Sammy is a busy little 7-year-old boy.

Despair and disappointment constantly bombard today's culture. Our personal crises may involve sickness, financial emergencies, losing a loved one, or countless other things. Natural calamities such as tsunamis, earthquakes, hurricanes, volcanoes, or floods overwhelm many.

Is there hope? Absolutely, yes!

What about hope for salvation? for overcoming sin? for daily provisions? for divine protection? for eternal life? We will consider all of these in this chapter.

World War I pilot Eddie Rickenbacker and seven friends survived in a raft for more than 20 days and nights without food or fresh water after their plane crashed in the Pacific during World Ware II. Miracles preserved them. When they were faint from thirst, a rainsquall blew up, providing fresh water. And when they were hungry, a seagull flew close enough so that they could catch it, eat it, and use part of its body to catch fish. After their rescue they were individually asked, "To whom do you attribute your survival?" All of them answered, "One of us brought a New Testament Bible that we read every day. The Bible gave us hope to live."

Yes, "we through the patience and comfort of the Scriptures might have hope" (Rom. 15:4, NKJV). Not only was Eddie Rickenbacker given hope to live—he was living with the hope of being saved. "Salvation" and "rescue" can be used interchangeably.

How important is hope for life? Dr. McNair Wilson, the famous cardiologist, remarked in his autobiography, *Doctor's Progress,* "Hope is the medicine I use more than any other—hope can cure nearly anything."[1] Yes, hope is vitally important in our human life. Dr. Harold Wolff, professor of medicine at Cornell University Medical College and associate professor of psychiatry, said, "Hope, like faith and a purpose in life, is medicinal. This is . . . a conclusion proved by meticulously controlled scientific experiment."[2]

Hope comes from a variety of places, such as another person's promise. The prisoners of war clung to MacArthur's words "I will return," and daily they hoped that he would come. And true to his promise, he did return and rescue them.

Faith in God offers hope. The Bible also offers hope through its hundreds of promises. Just one Bible text will suffice: "For everything that was written in the past was written to teach us, so that through endurance and the encouragement of the Scriptures we might have hope" (Rom. 15:4, NIV).

Hope of Salvation

The Bible emphasizes what we inherently know—that we all are sinners (Rom. 3:20) and that the wages of sin is death (Rom. 6:23). Paul expressed our human struggle for salvation when he said, "What a wretched man I am! Who will rescue me from this body of death?" (Rom. 7:24, NIV). He answered his own question in the next verse: "Thanks be to God—through Jesus Christ our Lord!" (verse 25, NIV). He also tells us that "the gift of God is eternal life in Christ Jesus our Lord (Rom. 6:23, NIV). Through Jesus we can experience hope! "For in this hope we were saved" (Rom. 8:24, NIV).

The Bible gives us hope for salvation and reconciliation with God through Jesus (Rom. 5:6-11). The hope promised to us by the Lord includes:

- restoration (1 Peter 3:18; Rom. 3:26).
- instruction in the way of salvation (John 16:13; 2 Tim. 3:16).
- conviction and the drawing power of Christ (John 12:32; 16:8).
- transformation and life (Rom. 1:16; Gal. 2:20).

- remission of sins (Acts 2:38).
- the gift of the Holy spirit, manifested in fruits of the Spirit (Acts 5:32; Gal. 5:22, 23).
- happiness (John 13:17).
- peace (John 14:27).

The Lord extends to us tremendous hope because the sinful nature of human beings requires large doses of it! God alone is the source of hope. The psalmist declares, "For you have been my hope, O Sovereign Lord, my confidence since my youth" (Ps. 71:5, NIV).

Although the plan of salvation will not be completed until sin is eradicated and the world is made new, all who have accepted Jesus can be free from guilt and experience peace of mind, joy, and happiness in their lives today.

Hope to Overcome Sin

The man at the Pool of Bethesda had been sick for 38 years (a span of time longer than many people lived during New Testament times) when Jesus met him. He felt hopeless. Listen to his plaintive reply to Jesus' question "Do you want to get well?"

"Sir," he replied, "I have no one to help me" (John 5:6, 7, NIV). Poor man—he was trusting in human help that had never come. How like him are we? Have you been trying to overcome some sin in your life all on your own or hoping for someone else to help you? Is it possible that people have come to church for years while having never been healed from the sickness of sin? Do you know people struggling to overcome their weakness against tobacco, alcohol, gambling, or pornography? Is there any hope for overcoming sin? Below are some steps, adapted from Alcoholics Anonymous and supported with Bible texts, that can give encouragement to struggling Christians.

1. I can't overcome in my own strength (John 15:5; Rom. 7:18).
2. But He can. A Power greater than I am can bring victory (Phil. 4:13; Eph. 3:20; Jude 24, 25).
3. I think I'll let Him. Surrendering my will and life to God unites my weakness with His strength (Matt. 26:39, 42; Luke 22:42).
4. Examining myself, I make a careful and fearless moral inventory of myself, searching for all character defects, not just the ones troubling me most (2 Cor. 13:5).

5. I admit my failures to God, to myself, and to other human beings (James 5:16; Gal. 6:1).
6. I become willing for God to remove my defects (Ps. 51:1, 2, 7).
7. I humbly submit to Him (verse 10).
8. I come to the conviction that a willingness to confess my sins must precede such a confession (Luke 15:17-19).
9. Then I make that confession—also making direct amends wherever possible to those I might have hurt (verse 21; 1 John 1:9).
10. I continue to take inventory of my life and admit wrongs in order to grow (Phil. 1:6; Ps. 139:23, 24).
11. I seek through prayer and meditation to improve my relationship with God (1 Thess. 5:17).
12. I share with others the message of forgiveness and victory (Mark 5:19, 20).

The hope of recovery from any addiction carries one over the rough spots. The "higher power" for the struggling Christian is Jesus. Letting Him take over the life is the only thing that brings success.

We need to realize that those who begin a new life in Jesus may fall, repeating the same mistake again and again, even as the alcoholic may "fall off the wagon." But the Bible says, "I can do everything through him who gives me strength" (Phil. 4:13, NIV) and "though a righteous man falls seven times, he rises again" (Prov. 24:16, NIV). John encourages," My dear children, I write this to you so that you will not sin. But if anybody does sin, we have one who speaks to the Father in our defense—Jesus Christ, the Righteous One" (1 John 2:1, NIV).

Although we may fall, we have hope that we will rise again. Jesus defends us as our mediator. The Bible says that through the power of Jesus we can overcome. "In all these things we are more than conquerors through him who loved us" (Rom. 8:37, NIV). (The entire eighth chapter of Romans is most encouraging.) That, my friend, is hope!

Two other things, not included in the Twelve Steps, are important:

- Destroy or throw away everything that might tempt you to fall into temptation. "Do not think about how to gratify the desires of the sinful nature" (Rom. 13:14, NIV).
- Continue praising the Lord for His great power to overcome your weaknesses. Praise Him for the victory that is already yours *in Christ Jesus*. "You, dear children, are from God and have overcome them,

because the one who is in you is greater than the one who is in the world" (1 John 4:4, NIV).

Hope for Daily Provision
We live in a hungry world.

- One hundred fifty children *die every day* from starvation in the United States of America alone.
- Around the world, 24,000 people perish every day from starvation.
- One out of every eight children less than 8 years old goes to bed hungry every night in the United States. It's far worse globally.
- More than 800 million people around the world are starving, and many are also homeless.
- More than 9 million people die worldwide each year because of hunger and malnutrition. Five million are children.[3]

People are looking for food. Is there any hope that they will be able to eat tomorrow? Can they obtain nourishment next week? The Bible speaks about the hope of salvation and eternal life, but is there hope for meeting our daily needs in this sinful world? The Bible gives us that kind of hope. Consider these: "The Lord is my shepherd; I shall want nothing" (Ps. 23:1, NEB). "Give us this day our daily bread" (Matt. 6:11). God fed the Israelites in the wilderness (Ex. 16:4), and He also took care of Elijah and Elisha (1 Kings 19:3-9; 2 Kings 2:9-14). Those who look to God to provide their daily needs can trust His goodness.

God, the Creator of the whole universe, loves His creatures. Paul says, "Do not be anxious about anything, but in everything, by prayer and petition, with thanksgiving, present your requests to God" (Phil. 4:6, NIV). The Bible says that He not only provides our daily needs, but in many cases bestows on His people such riches that they can serve as channels of blessings to others, helping to alleviate suffering.

Hope for Divine Protection
We live in an unsafe world with its tragedies, terrorism, and "wars and rumours of wars" (Matt. 24:6). "Men will faint from terror, apprehensive of what is coming on the world" (Luke 21:26, NIV). Is there any safe place in our world?

The Bible says "Yes!" David, who survived many trials, said, "Even though I walk through the valley of the shadow of death, I will fear no evil, for you are with me; your rod and your staff they comfort me" (Ps. 23:4, NIV). As with David, we need not fear as long as we know that God is with us. The Hebrew word *salmavet* is a compound noun that means "valley of death" or "gates of death" (cf. Job 38:17). Jeremiah 2:6 uses the same term to describe the perils of the desert. It points to a wide range of crises: pain, perplexity, and frustration as a result of an uncertain future. God has promised that He will be with us when we are facing difficulties.

The Bible uses the phrase "fear not" more than 50 times. We should not have any fear at all.

The psalmist, in full confidence of God's protection, said: "God is our refuge and strength, an ever-present help in trouble. Therefore we will not fear, though the earth give way and the mountains fall into the heart of the sea, though its waters roar and foam and the mountains quake with their surging" (Ps. 46:1-3, NIV). "The angel of the Lord encamps around those who fear him, and he delivers them" (Ps. 34:7, NIV). "He will cover you with his feathers, and under his wings you will find refuge; his faithfulness will be your shield and rampart" (Ps. 91:4, NIV). "As the mountains surround Jerusalem, so the Lord surrounds his people both now and forevermore" (Ps. 125:2, NIV).

Even though the Bible promises God's protection from harm and danger, we still see His people suffer. Why? Perhaps He has a special purpose in allowing us to experience difficulties in our lives. Romans 5:3-5 reminds us that "tribulation produces perseverance; and perseverance, character; and character, hope" (NKJV). When we get to heaven, we can ask Jesus to explain His purpose in allowing our trials.

Hope of Everlasting Life

David exclaimed, "May those who fear you rejoice when they see me, for I have put my hope in your word" (Ps. 119:74, NIV). He also said, "You are my refuge and my shield; I have put my hope in your word" (verse 114, NIV). Both texts show the power of the Word of God to produce hope in our life. This hope includes the promise of everlasting life.

Everlasting life actually begins in this world when we know God (John 17:3), and it extends forever! Jesus Himself promised: "Let not your heart be troubled; you believe in God, believe also in Me. In My Father's house are many mansions; if it were not so, I would have told you. I go to prepare a place for you. And if I go and prepare a place for you, I will come again and receive you to Myself; that where I am, there you may be also" (John 14:1-3, NKJV).

Notice the last part of His promise. Did He say "Perhaps I'll come again" or "I'm not sure, but I'll think about it"? No! Jesus declared with the full force and honesty of His character, *I will come again.* There is no uncertainty about His returning again "to receive us to Himself." Now notice an additional aspect of His promise: "I will come again and receive you to *Myself; that where I am, there you may be also.*" He is in heaven, preparing a place for us, and He will come to take us to be where He is. Christ will catch us up in the clouds to meet Him! His second advent will be a very real event. It will be literal, personal, tangible—and cataclysmic.

When Jesus returns, He will resurrect the righteous dead and translate the still-living righteous. Then we shall all live together with Him forever.

Even in our hopeless world death is not the end of life. The grave is not our loved one's final resting place. Nor is it a prison from which there's no deliverance. Jesus Christ went into the grave and came out triumphant over death. As the Life-giver, He raised Lazarus from the dead, giving positive proof that those who love Him will be resurrected when He comes. The hope of eternal life includes the resurrection of the dead (1 Thess. 4:14-17). God gives us hope that we will live forever in a place where there will be no sorrow, no sickness, and no suffering (Rev. 21).

Our hope goes beyond just a desire to live forever. It includes the promise that sins will be eradicated. Listen to these beautiful words: "The great controversy is ended. Sin and sinners are no more. The entire universe is clean. One pulse of harmony and gladness beats through the vast creation. From Him who created all flow life and light and gladness, throughout the realms of illimitable space. From the minutest atom to the greatest world, all things, animate and inanimate, in their unshadowed beauty and perfect joy, declare that God is love."[4]

Summary

People do not know what will happen in the future, but we have learned that God promises us hope. Even in the midst of daily suffering, sickness, agony, starvation, and sorrow, we can have hope. Such hope helps us not to worry about tomorrow, because we know who controls it. God provides for our daily needs. He protects us from harm and danger. And He assures us of everlasting life in the world made new, where there will be no more sickness, separation, or death.

Our loving Father, in His love letter to us, gives us hope enough so that we can endure to the end.

¹ In Billy Graham, *Hope for the Troubled Heart* (Dallas: Word Publishing, 1991), p. ix.
² *Ibid.*
³ UNICEF statistics for 2002.
⁴ E. G. White, *The Great Controversy,* p. 678.

CHAPTER 9

The Bible Makes Us Healthy

Today more than ever, people are health-conscious. We hear about weight-control programs, miracle drugs, dietary supplements, and exercise. People want good health. God longs for us to enjoy life with as little suffering as possible (3 John 2). The current worldwide interest in health provides us opportunities to introduce biblical principles of good health to others.

Too often people recognize the need for good health only when it is too late! Dr. H. E. Kirschner wrote the following poem, found in the book *Toward a Healthy Lifestyle:*

> "We squander health in search of wealth,
> We scheme, and toil and save.
> Then squander wealth in search of health
> And all we get's a grave.
> We live and boast of what we own;
> We die, and only get a stone." [1]

In this chapter we will discuss how to achieve a healthy lifestyle so we can serve the Lord better, maintain an alert mind and spiritual life, and enjoy good relationships with others.

Recognizing that a healthy body is important for all of life, we ask, "How can we achieve it? How can we handle daily stress?" Dr. Harold G. Koenig, author of *Is Religion Good for Your Health?* tells of a Mrs. Bernard, one of his patients. She had lost her only son in a tragic car accident six months prior to meeting Dr. Koenig. Then, five weeks before, her husband had died suddenly. A week after that, while attending his funeral, she had slipped on the ice and fractured her hip. During her recovery from the hip fracture, she had developed a severe lung infection that required a prolonged stay in the hospital.

When Dr. Koenig walked into Mrs. Bernard's room, he found her reading the Bible. She told him that it helped her handle the stress in her life. "Whenever I get to feeling sad or blue, I pick up my Bible and begin reading it, and somehow this calms me," she said. "When I wake up at night and feel alone or afraid, I read my Bible or talk to God. He's always there, even when my family and friends are not."[2]

The Bible Wants Us to Be Healthy

The Bible gives at least seven reasons we should keep healthy.

1. We are God's creatures. The first two chapters of Genesis show that He created heaven, earth, and human beings. As His creatures, we need to follow the Creator's formula for a healthy lifestyle.

2. We owe it to our own body. Ephesians 5:29 says, "For no one ever hated his own flesh, but nourishes and cherishes it, just as the Lord does the church" (NKJV). Observe those who own a new car. They spend time washing it on a regular basis and making sure that the oil gets changed at the scheduled time. Why do they put so much effort into maintaining it? Because they own it. So it is with our own bodies. When we care for them, they will give us years of good service, allowing us to enjoy life and the pursuit of happiness.

3. We owe it to our family. When a person is sick, it is likely that the illness will affect others as well. For one thing, another person must care for him or her, increasing the risk of the caregiver's becoming ill, especially if the sickness is an infectious disease. Furthermore, the extra care given the sick person takes time and attention away from the rest of the family. Should the sick person die, grief will devastate family and friends. No wonder the Bible says, "For none of us lives to himself, and no one dies to himself" (Rom. 14:7, NKJV).

4. We owe it to God. Under principle 2 above, we suggested that we own our bodies. But do we really? First Corinthians 6:19, 20, says: "Do you not know that your body is the temple of the Holy Spirit who is in you, whom you have from God, and you are not your own? For you were bought at a price; therefore glorify God in your body and in your spirit, which are God's" (NKJV). Our bodies belong not to us, but to our Redeemer. Because we have been purchased with the blood of Jesus, we should glorify God through our bodies. Obviously we can do that better with healthy bodies than with sickly ones.

5. If we destroy our body, God will destroy us. First Corinthians 3:16, 17, declares: "Do you not know that you are the temple of God . . . ? If anyone defiles the temple of God, God will destroy him. For the temple of God is holy, which temple you are" (NKJV).

At first glance it makes the Lord sound extremely vengeful. Is it not rather that we *destroy ourselves?* How can we glorify God with our bodies instead of hurting them? First Corinthians 10:31 says: "Therefore, whether you eat or drink, or whatever you do, do all to the glory of God" (NKJV). By carefully monitoring what we eat and drink, and by avoiding anything that would injure our health, we honor Him.

6. *A healthy body is our sacrifice to God.* "Therefore, I urge you, brothers, in view of God's mercy, to offer your bodies as living sacrifices, holy and pleasing to God—this is your spiritual act of worship" (Rom. 12:1, NIV). Because God instructed the Israelites to offer only perfect sacrifices to Him (Ex. 12:5), we as spiritual Israelites need also to offer only the best sacrifice—our healthy bodies.

7. *People are wholistic beings.* "Dear friend, I pray that you may enjoy good health and that all may go well with you, even as your soul is getting along well" (3 John 2, NIV). Jeremiah tells us that the Lord, the source of health, will restore us to health and heal our wounds (Jer. 30:17). We need to be healthy physically, mentally, and spiritually. In many cases our physical health depends upon our spiritual and mental health, since our spiritual and mental outlook influences our physical condition.

Human Wholeness

Sin affects every aspect of life. However, God plans to restore us to Adam's original state. "All that was lost by the first Adam will be restored by the second."[3] God's redemption will include the whole being.

We can see His concern for our physical, mental, and spiritual restoration as we examine the way He guides His people and the kind of commandments He proclaims. Some commandments, given to improve spiritual life, also involve our physical nature. For example, God's instruction to Abraham to circumcise all the members of his household (Gen. 17:10-12, 14) represented a spiritual relationship with God. However, medical science offers evidence that circumcision also has physical health aspects. According to Stanley Robbins, in his textbook on general pathology, "the ritual of circumcision as practiced by the Hebrews during the first two weeks of life has for all purposes virtually eliminated carcinoma of the penis."[4] Thus, when God gave His commandments in the Bible, He had in mind both our *spiritual* and our *physical* well-being.

This shows the interrelation between obedience to the law of God and

77

physical health. In Exodus 15:26 the Lord promised the Israelites physical blessings on condition that they obey His laws. But if they disobeyed His commandments, He warned that He would send curses, confusion, and diseases upon them (Deut. 28:20, 21).

Paul addressed the interrelationship between the physical, mental, and spiritual nature, saying: "And the very God of peace sanctify you wholly; and I pray God your whole spirit and soul and body be preserved blameless unto the coming of our Lord Jesus Christ" (1 Thess. 5:23). We humans are indivisible. In Ellen White's words, "Bible sanctification has to do with the whole man." [5]

Good Health Habits

Christ's followers should never say, "What I eat and drink or how I treat my body is my own business." We saw earlier that we should glorify God by what we eat and drink. Specific biblical instructions tell us how to care for our bodies, because their condition has a close connection to our spiritual well-being.

1. Dietary guidelines. The Bible gives specific guidance for foods. The original diet consisted of fruits and nuts (Gen. 1:29), and the adapted diet after the Fall included vegetables (Gen. 3:18).

In the 2005 *Dietary Guidelines for Americans,* the U.S. Department of Agriculture states that vegetarians of all types can achieve recommended nutrient intakes through careful selection of foods.[6] Fruits, vegetables, and whole grains protect our health. The key to eating a balanced plant-based diet is to include a variety of foods that have good color, texture, and flavor. Dietitians sometimes refer to this as the rainbow-colored diet. Often the deeper the colors of the food, the more protective their value is against cancer and heart disease.[7]

2. The need for sufficient water. The Bible tells of the Great Shepherd who "leads me beside the still waters" (Ps. 23:2, NKJV), thus reflecting His care in meeting our need for water. Water is a vital element for life. An adult's total body weight consists of 70 percent water. The gray matter of the brain is 85 percent water, the blood is 83 percent water, the muscles contain 75 percent water, and even the marrow of bones consists of 20 to 25 percent water.[8] Water surrounds the cells of the body, and they require water to perform their functions. Many conditions, including headache, kidney stones, gallstones, heart attack, and even death, develop because of dehydration.[9] We can truly say that without water there cannot be good health.

3. The need for rest. Jesus invited His disciples to rest for a while (Mark

6:31). Rest is vital for every individual. Scientific discoveries show that people deprived of sufficient sleep have lower immunity, resulting in diseases ranging from runny noses to cancer.[10]

Drs. Nedra Belloc and Lester Breslow were among the first researchers to present convincing evidence that certain lifestyle factors can lead to longer life. In their classic study of 6,928 adult residents of Alameda County, California, they found that adequate sleep was one of the seven lifestyle factors that influenced how long people lived. Persons obtaining eight to nine hours of sleep per night have better health than do those getting either shorter or longer periods.[11]

Loss of sleep is a major stressor affecting our mental life (impairing memory), emotional life (producing anger or frustration), social life (causing difficulty in getting along with others), and our physical life (depressing the immune system and lowering the body's resistance to colds or flu).[12] Loss of sleep causes reduced efficiency and productivity and impaired judgment, making a person more prone to accidents. God truly loves us and stresses the need to have sufficient rest to avoid negative impacts on our physical, mental, emotional, and social life.

4. The need for exercise. When the Lord asked Adam and Eve to take care of the Garden of Eden, He wanted them to do work that involved exercise. A Harvard alumni study showed that active people are sick less often, have more energy, are more successful at weight management, cope better with stress and pressure, and have less depression and a more positive self-image.[13] The Centers for Disease Control and Prevention and the American College of Sports Medicine recommend that every U.S. adult should accumulate 30 minutes or more of moderately intense physical activity on most (preferably all) days of the week.[14] God certainly loves us and wants us to exercise on a regular basis for our own good.

5. The need for temperance. The fruit of the Spirit includes temperance (Gal. 5:23). Ellen White gives the best definition for temperance that we can find: "True temperance teaches us to dispense entirely with everything hurtful and to use judiciously that which is healthful."[15] While we need to avoid the use of tobacco, alcohol, drugs, or anything else harmful to the body, at the same time we must avoid excesses in *healthful* practices. That might include our food intake or too much exercise, work, and sleep.

For example, sleeping is good, but too much can be detrimental to your health. E. C. Hammond discovered that the lowest death rate was in those men averaging around seven hours of sleep per night, whereas those who either skimped on their sleep or spent too much time in bed died at a younger age than those who got the proper amount on a regular basis.[16] God truly wants us to practice temperance even in our rest habits.

A Healthy Environment

God in His love provided us with a healthy environment. Fresh air and sunlight are two vital gifts that the Lord created. Without light there can be no life; and without air we could not survive more than a few minutes. Both are vital to life.

Through photosynthesis, plants use energy from sunlight to combine carbon dioxide from the air and water from the soil to make food. During the process plants give off oxygen. We eat the plants and breathe the oxygen they release. Then we exhale carbon dioxide that the plants require. Sunshine provides us with many benefits:

- It stimulates the production of vitamin D.
- It helps the body to build and repair bones.
- It kills many bacteria, viruses, and molds.
- It influences the production of serotonin, which may in turn prevent depression and fatigue.

Dr. Mark Levy, chair of the San Francisco Foundation for Psychoanalysis, says, "For those with mild cases [of seasonal affective disorder, a type of major seasonal depression with many symptoms of clinical depression], 30 minutes of exercise out in the morning sun may be all that is needed to keep the winter blues at bay."[17]

We need good fresh air for life and for health. Today's pollution problems make finding clear air a challenge, especially in cities and industrial areas. Ellen White admonishes us, "In order to have good blood, we must breathe well. Full, deep inspirations of pure air, which fill the lungs with oxygen, purify the blood. They impart to it a bright color and send it, a life-giving current, to every part of the body. A good respiration soothes the nerves; it stimulates the appetite and renders digestion more perfect; and it induces sound, refreshing sleep."[18] The key to full utilization of the lungs is to exercise regularly. Even during work or study time, we need to pause and breathe deeply, particularly fresh air (outdoors preferably), in order to recharge our body and brain function.

A Healthy Mind

Long before the scientific discovery of the relationship between mind and body, the Bible declared: "For as he thinks in his heart, so is he" (Prov. 23:7, NKJV). This text shows the importance of the mind's influence on the total person. Everyone has a choice in any situation whether to be happy or sad, to have peace or worry. We choose our attitudes. Scripture teaches us to be positive and optimistic rather than negative or pessimistic in facing life's challenges. Jesus said that we should not worry about anything (Matt. 6:25-34). Thus we should not worry about our food, clothes, or even our future. Instead, as Paul pointed out, we need to have joy in our life (Phil. 4:4-8). Does science support the concept of having a positive outlook?

Scientific discovery shows that negative emotions will trigger the release of certain hormones and stimulate the nervous system in such a way as to put stress on the various organs of the body. After enduring the strain for a long time, they become weakened and more susceptible to disease. How it will affect the organs depends on a person's heredity, constitution, environment, and lifestyle.[19] John Marks reported in the December 11, 1995, issue of *U.S. News & World Report* that "somewhere between 75 and 90 percent of all doctor's visits" stem from stress.[20] Ellen White said exactly the same thing 150 years ago: "Sickness of the mind prevails everywhere. Nine tenths of the diseases from which man suffers have their foundation here."[21]

On the other hand, happiness and genuine laughter activate the sympathetic nervous system to produce catecholamines, which then trigger the anterior pituitary lobe to manufacture endorphins. The latter are natural painkillers, and they also increase the activity of the immune cells. Laughter is a powerful medicine.

God wants us to be healthy physically, mentally, and spiritually. A healthy mind results in part from peaceful thoughts. What is our source of peaceful thoughts? Isaiah long ago said: "You will keep him in perfect peace, whose mind is stayed on You: because he trusts in You" (Isa. 26:3, NKJV). It is God who gives us healthy minds and perfect peace, as we trust Him fully.

One of the meanings of the word "stay" in *Webster's New World Dictionary* is "to keep, to remain." Therefore, we could read the above text as "You will keep him in perfect peace whose mind *remains or stays* with You." When we have our mind focused on the Lord, He gives us perfect peace.

Healthy Relationships

Again and again the Bible speaks about our need for loving one another. Jesus said that love is the greatest of all the commandments (Matt.

22:37-40) and that a significant characteristic of His followers is that they love another (John 13:35). Paul, speaking about Christian virtues, said that love is greater than faith or hope (1 Cor. 13:13). *The Interpreter's Bible* observes that "where there is no obvious ground for faith it [love] continues to hope; where there is no apparent ground for hope it continues to endure. Love is like an army that is threatened with overwhelming defeat by superior numbers of the enemy but steadfastly refuses to give ground." [22]

We live in a sick world. In some countries family violence is a major public health crisis. In the United States "38 percent of girls and 17.3 percent of boys experience sexual abuse prior to the age of eighteen. Violent attacks by men constitute the greatest health risk to women in this country where an estimated 3 to 4 million women are battered each year by their husbands or partners." [23]

The numbers of drug addicts and juvenile delinquents continue to increase. How can we, as a church, the body of Christ, contribute to the welfare of our families, congregations, community, and society as a whole? The National Longitudinal Study on Adolescent Health, which involved thousands of teenagers and parents across the United States, reveals that adolescents who are connected to their parents, to their families, and to their school are protected from many risk behaviors, such as sex, violence, emotional distress, suicidal attempts, and drug use. [24]

The Bible spoke of connectedness in the church family long ago. As God's people we need to:

- love one another (John 15:12; 1 Peter 1:22; 1 John 3:23).
- serve one another (Gal. 5:13).
- forbear one another (Eph. 4:2).
- be kind to one another (verse 32).
- edify or build up one another (Rom. 4:19).
- admonish or instruct one another (Rom. 15:14).
- be tenderhearted and forgiving to one another (Eph. 4:32).
- encourage one another (1 Thess. 4:18).
- show compassion or sympathy to one another (1 Peter 3:8).
- be hospitable to one another (1 Peter 4:9).
- pray for one another (James 5:16).

These "one another commands," so clearly outlined by the Word, will help us become connected to one another, will strengthen family relationships, and will ultimately protect our youth from many high-risk behaviors.

Gleaning from the Bible, Ellen G. White books, and medical science, the General Conference Health Ministries Department compiled several proven practices that ensure the best possible health. They expressed them through the acronym CELEBRATIONS:

C is for Choices—the cradle of your destiny.

E is for Exercise—the elixir of your energy.

L is for Liquids—the lubricant of your functionality.

E is for Environment—the empowerment of your community.

B is for Belief—the basis of your spirituality.

R is for Rest—the restorer of your resiliency.

A is for Air—the activator of your vitality.

T is for Temperance—the temple of your purity.

I is for Integrity—the incorruptibility of your honesty.

O is for Optimism—the operant of your sanity.

N is for Nutrition—the nourishment of your body.

S is for Social Support and Service—the stewardship of your relationships.

The Bible does indeed provide guidelines for a healthy lifestyle.

Summary

The Bible clearly gives us principles for physical, mental, and spiritual health. By following them, we can enjoy life. The Creator, who knows what is best for His children, wants us to be healthy. That is why He gave us His "owner's manual," His love letter, the Bible, that tells us how to maintain vibrant health.

---

[1] In Albert Hutapea, *Toward Healthy Lifestyle* (Jakarta: Penerbit PT Gramedia Pustake Utama, 1993), p. v.

[2] Harold G. Koenig, M.D., *Is Religion Good for Your Health?* (Binghamton, N.Y.: Haworth Press, 1997), pp. 5, 6.

[3] E. G. White, *Patriarchs and Prophets*, p. 67.

[4] In Harvey Rosenstock, "On the Genesis of Public Health: One Facet of Pentateuchal Materia Medica," *Arizona Medicine*, May 25, 1967, p. 494.

[5] Ellen G. White, *Counsels on Health* (Mountain View, Calif.: Pacific Press Pub. Assn., 1923), p.

[6] Judith E. Brown, *Dietary Guidelines for Americans* (Belmont, Calif.: Wadsworth Pub. Co., 2005), p. 9.

[7] http://www.helpguide.org/life/healthy_diet_cancer_prevention.html.

[8] M. G. Hardinge, *A Philosophy of Health* (Loma Linda, Calif.: School of Health, Loma

Linda University, 1980), p. 37.

[9] R. H. Grimm, Jr., J. D. Neaton, and W. Ludwig, "Prognostic Importance of the White Blood Cell Count for Coronary, Cancer, and All-cause Mortality," *Journal of the American Medical Association* 254, no. 14 (Oct. 11, 1985): 1932-1937.

[10] http://www.nhlbi.nih.gov/health/prof/sleep/sleep99.html.

[11] Nedra Belloc and Lester Breslow, "Relationship of Physical Health Status and Health Practices," *Preventive Medicine* 1, no. 3 (August 1972): 409-421.

[12] *Ibid.*

[13] www.news.harvard.edu/gazette/2001/05.31/01-exercise.html.

[14] R. R. Pate et al., "Physical Activity and Public Health," *Journal of American Medical Association* 273, no. 5 (Feb. 1, 1995): 402-407.

[15] White, *Patriarchs and Prophets,* p. 562.

[16] E. C. Hammond, "Some Preliminary Findings on Physical Complaints From a Prospective Study of 1,064,004 Men and Women," *American Journal of Public Health* 54 (1964): 22, 23.

[17] In Chris Cosgrove, "The Blue Season," Jan. 3, 2000; www.cnn.com/2000/HEALTH/01/03/sad.wmd.

[18] Ellen G. White, *The Ministry of Healing* (Mountain View, Calif.: Pacific Press Pub. Assn., 1904), p. 272.

[19] M. H. Beers, A. J. Fletcher, T. V. Jones, R. Porter, M. Berkwits, J. L. Kaplan, *The Merck Manual of Medical Information* (Whitehouse Station, N.J.: Merck Research Laboratories Division of Merck and Co., Inc., 2003), pp. 6-8.

[20] John Marks, in *U.S. News & World Report,* Dec. 11, 1995, p. 90.

[21] E. G. White, *Testimonies,* vol. 5, p. 444.

[22] *The Interpreter's Bible* (New York: Abingdon Press, 1953), vol. 10, pp. 184, 185.

[23] N. J. Ramsay, "Confronting Family Violence and Its Spiritual Damage," *Family Ministry* 13, no. 3 (Fall 1999): 46, 47.

[24] R. W. Blum and P. M. Rinehart, "Reducing the Risk: Connections That Make a Difference in the Lives of Youth" (Minneapolis: Division of Adolescent Health and Development, Division of General Pediatrics and Adolescent Health, University of Minnesota, undated). Based on the first analysis of Add Health data, M. D. Resnick et al.,"Protecting Adolescents From Harm: Findings From the National Longitudinal Study on Adolescent Health," *Journal of the American Medical Association,* 278, no. 10 (Sept. 10, 1997): 823-832.

CHAPTER 10

The Bible Makes Us Happy

A Mr. Speed, who was a friend of Abraham Lincoln's, on one occasion found the president reading his Bible. Not a fan of formal religion, the man challenged Lincoln. "If you have recovered from your skepticism, I am sorry," he said, "but I have not." To which Lincoln replied, "You are wrong, Speed. Take all of this Book on reason that you can, and the balance on faith, and you will live and die a happier man."[1]

God wants you and me to be happy, and the Bible is a guide that will make it possible for us. Especially in the New Testament the word "blessed" often has the connotation of being "happy." Thus on one occasion Jesus said, "Blessed [happy] . . . are those who hear the word of God and obey it" (Luke 11:28, NIV). Near the end of His life He proclaimed, "Now that you know these things, you will be blessed [happy] if you do them" (John 13:17, NIV). And in the Beatitudes (Matt. 5:3-11) Jesus gave nine principles for Christian happiness.

The apostle John explained that the purpose of his first letter was "to make your joy complete" (1 John 1:4, margin, NIV). And in the Old Testament Isaiah promised that in heaven the redeemed "will enter Zion with singing; everlasting joy will crown their heads. Gladness and joy will overtake them, and sorrow and sighing will flee away" (Isa. 35:10, NIV).

The Psalms contain numerous references to rejoicing in God and His salvation. Here are several examples:

- "We will rejoice in your salvation" (Ps. 20:5, NKJV).
- "In Your salvation how greatly shall he [the king] rejoice!" (Ps. 21:1, NKJV).
- "I will be glad and rejoice in your love" (Ps. 31:7, NIV).
- "Rejoice in the Lord, . . . you righteous" (Ps. 32:11, NIV).

- "My soul will rejoice in the Lord and delight in his salvation" (Ps. 35:9, NIV).

It's true: *God wants you to be happy!* And He has provided His Word to guide you into that happiness. Let's find out how the Bible can make us happy.

Peace
One of the characteristics of genuine happiness is peace of mind. Happiness cannot exist without it. David said, "The Lord blesses his people with peace" (Ps. 29:11, NIV), and he advised, "Seek peace and pursue it" (Ps. 34:14, NIV). Isaiah promised that God will keep us "in perfect peace" (Isa. 26:3). In the New Testament the angels who proclaimed Jesus' birth said, "On earth peace, good will toward men" (Luke 2:14). "Peace I leave with you, my peace I give unto you," Jesus told us (John 14:27). And Paul began nearly all of his letters with the words: "Grace and peace to you" (Rom. 1:7, NIV; 1 Cor. 1:3, NIV; Gal. 1:3, NIV, etc.).

One of humanity's quests throughout the ages has been to find peace with God. Non-Christians as well as Christians feel guilt over their sins and imperfections, and they want to know that they are in right relation with Him. In ancient times pagans tried to find such peace by offering sacrifices to their gods. The Bible mentions some of those deities: "Ashtoreth the goddess of the Sidonians, Chemosh the god of the Moabites, and Molech the god of the Ammonites" (1 Kings 11:33, NIV). Molech was a particularly reprehensible deity, because people offered human sacrifices, sometimes even children, to it (Jer. 32:35). That's the extreme that some have gone to in order to feel at peace with their gods.

Christians have a much better way to find peace with the true God. Paul said, "Therefore, since we have been justified through faith, we have *peace with God* through our Lord Jesus Christ" (Rom. 5:1, NIV). So Christians find peace with Him through what the Bible calls "justification," a gift that we receive through Jesus. But what is this justification that brings peace with God?

All other religions in the world seek to please God through the adherent's good deeds. But the Lord knows that nothing on our part can atone for our sins. Therefore, Jesus came to this earth, lived a perfect life, and atoned for our sins Himself by dying for them. Now, in the words of Ellen White, "He offers to take our sins and give us His righteousness." The Lord *gives* us the righteousness we need in order to stand perfect before

Him. In fact, Ellen White went on to say that "Christ's character stands in place of [our] character, and [we] are accepted before God just as if [we] had not sinned"![2] To be accepted before God "just as if [we] had not sinned" means that God regards us just as if we were perfect. Even in our imperfection God counts us as if we had not sinned.

Paul told us that "now a righteousness from God . . . has been made known" (Rom. 3:21, NIV). He meant that since we have no righteousness to offer God, He personally offers us the righteousness that we need in order to be acceptable to Him. In Philippians 3:9 the apostle stated that he wanted to "be found in him [Christ], not having a righteousness of my own that comes from [keeping] the law, but that which is through faith in Christ—the righteousness that comes from God and is by faith" (NIV). No wonder Paul said that justification leads to "peace with God"! Once we've been justified, we don't have to worry about the sins we've committed. God loves us and welcomes us just as we are.

That doesn't mean, of course, that we can sit back and relax and ignore our sins and character defects. God wants us to put forth efforts to overcome them. But even they aren't what qualify us for His approval. He accepts us on the basis of Christ's righteousness, never our own.

Trust

Of course, as Christians living in an imperfect world, we know that we won't always feel exuberant. It's easy to understand why Jesus said that the merciful, the pure in heart, and the peacemakers will be happy (Matt. 5:7-9). But it's harder to grasp why He said, "Blessed [happy] are those who mourn" (verse 4, NIV), or "Blessed [happy] are those who are persecuted" (verse 10, NIV). Life does have its griefs and sorrows, yet even in suffering and sadness we can find happiness.

James made a very significant comment about joy: "Consider it pure joy, my brothers, whenever you face trials of many kinds" (James 1:2, NIV). And Paul wrote to the Christians in Rome that "we also rejoice in our sufferings, because we know that suffering produces perseverance; perseverance, character; and character, hope. And hope does not disappoint us, because God has poured out his love into our hearts by the Holy Spirit, whom he has given us" (Rom. 5:3-6).

How can the Christian be happy when he or she is suffering? A concept that Paul shared in Romans 8:28 helps us to understand: "And we know that in all things God works for the good of those who love him, who have been called according to his purpose" (NIV). It may be difficult to see how the circumstances in your life right now could possibly lead to anything good. Perhaps you've lost a dear friend or loved one in death. Maybe you've contracted a serious illness or suffered a major accident that has incapacitated you for a period of time. One cannot imagine how such trials could possibly help us in any way. And, in fact, in some cases we may have to wait till resurrection day to understand. Our angel will have to explain the meaning of our sorrow in heaven. But when he does, we will see how every trial on this earth truly did work for our good.

Philippians is the most joyful letter Paul ever wrote. He used the word "rejoice" nine times and "joy" seven times. Here are three examples:

- "Even if I am being poured out as a drink offering on the sacrifice and service coming from your faith, I am glad and rejoice with all of you" (Phil. 2:17, NIV).
- "I rejoice. And I will continue to rejoice" (Phil. 1:18, NLT).
- "Rejoice in the Lord always. I will say it again: Rejoice! (Phil. 4:4, NIV).

Now, here's the amazing thing about those statements: Paul composed his letter to the Christians in Philippi while he was in prison—yet he expressed joy! He was a prime example of a Christian who found joy in the midst of suffering and who could declare, "We also rejoice in our sufferings, because we know that suffering produces perseverance; perseverance, character; and character, hope. And hope does not disappoint us, because God has poured out his love into our hearts by the Holy Spirit, whom he has given us" (Rom. 5:3-5, NIV).

So how can a Christian rejoice in sufferings? The answer is simple: When we can't see how "in all things God works for our good," we must still *trust* that it's true. That's why the Old Testament prophet Isaiah said, "You will keep him in perfect peace, whose mind is stayed on You, because he trusts in You" (Isa. 26:3, NKJV). Those who trust in God experience peace, and that brings them great joy.

Sometimes we *are* able to see the benefits of our suffering in this life, particularly when it has resulted from our own mistakes. Thus mistakes, and even the sins we commit, can become stepping-stones to victory and eventually a cause for rejoicing. Ellen White said, "If you have made mistakes, you certainly gain a victory if you see these mistakes and regard them as beacons of warning. Thus you turn defeat into victory, disappointing the enemy and honoring your Redeemer."[3] So the next time you experience defeat in your battle with temptation, instead of wallowing in guilt for an hour, a day, or maybe longer, ask God to forgive you and rejoice that you are indeed forgiven. Then request Him to show you what lesson you might discover from the incident that would help you to avoid yielding next time. Whatever you learn from the situation is a cause for rejoicing. And as you put it into practice and find that it helps you to gain more victories, you have even more cause for rejoicing. Here is one of the important ways the Bible interacts with your Christian experience to bring you happiness.

Someone once said, "A crisis is a dangerous opportunity." The opportunity aspect is that a crisis gives you a chance to grow in your Christian experience. It may also launch you into greater success in your career or your marriage. The danger is that you may respond to the crisis in the wrong way and cause yourself even greater pain. Are you facing a difficult situation in your life that's disturbing your peace? Consider it an opportunity to grow. And one good way to do that is to ask God to lead you through the crisis successfully, and then trust that He will.

Summary

The Bible is full of joy, and it can bring great happiness to our lives, even in the midst of suffering. We can have peace in the knowledge that Jesus is our Savior, that He accepts us and gives us His righteousness. Also we can rejoice that He gives us victory over our sins. And most of all, we can even praise our sufferings as we learn to trust God with the outcome.

---

[1] In C. L. Paddock, *God's Minutes* (Nashville: Southern Pub. Assn., 1965), p. 72.

[2] Ellen G. White, *Steps to Christ* (Mountain View, Calif.: Pacific Press Pub. Assn., 1956), p. 62.

[3] White, *Christ's Object Lessons*, p. 332.

CHAPTER 11

The Bible Makes Us Wise

Walter B. Knight, the author of *Knight's Treasury of Illustrations,* tells of one of his students who served as the navigator on a bomber during World War II. The younger man said that guiding his plane across the uncharted oceans was a simple matter. "Why, all I had to do was take a couple looks at the stars, and then look in a book. That book would tell me right where we were, making it the easiest thing in the world to get to our destination!" [1]

The Bible is like that. It shows us Jesus, "the . . . morning star" (Rev. 22:16), and it provides us with wisdom and guidance on how to live in this world. It tells us "right where we are" in our journey toward heaven while helping us to reach that destination safely. In fact, the Bible makes the stupendous claim that it is the source of wisdom (Prov. 2:6).

The Bible says that Solomon was the wisest man the world has ever known (1 Kings 4:30). He was so renowned for his wisdom that people from all over that part of the world came to him for advice (verse 34). The queen of Sheba arrived to check out his wisdom, and after spending several days with him she exclaimed, "Not even half was told me; in wisdom and wealth you have far exceeded the report I heard" (1 Kings 10:7, NIV). But where did he get his wisdom? The Bible says that "God gave Solomon wisdom and very great insight, and a breadth of understanding as measureless as the sand on the seashore" (1 Kings 4:29, NIV). Later in his life the king wrote, "The Lord gives wisdom, and from his mouth come knowledge and understanding" (Prov. 2:6, NIV). "Wisdom," Solomon said, "is more precious than rubies, and nothing you desire can compare with her" (Prov. 8:11, NIV). No wonder he also advised, "Get wisdom" (Prov. 4:5).

In his search for wisdom Solomon started exactly where you and I must when we sense the need of wisdom: He asked God for it. Shortly after his nation anointed Solomon king, the Lord came to him one night in a dream and said, "Ask for whatever you want me to give you" (2 Chron. 1:7, NIV). "Give me wisdom and knowledge, that I may lead this people, for who is able to govern this great people of yours?" Solomon replied (verse 10, NIV).

The king didn't request wisdom just so he could be a smart man. He needed it in order to carry out his duties as king of Israel. And he obtained that wisdom in the same way that you and I can get it: he requested it. The Bible promises, "If any of you lacks wisdom, he should ask God, who gives generously to all without finding fault, and it will be given to him" (James 1:5, NIV). So whatever your present responsibilities, the Lord will provide you wisdom to manage them well. Are you a student who needs to get good grades? Do you want it in order to serve your employer well? Are you facing a crisis that seems to have no solution? For each of these and a thousand other reasons, go to God for wisdom. He'll give it to you.

The Bible is the source of all spiritual wisdom. It's a practical guide for everyday life. The various chapters in this book reflect different aspects of wisdom that the Bible provides for us. However, let's examine two areas of life for which we all need wisdom, and with which we have not dealt to any great extent anywhere else: wisdom regarding the plan of salvation and wisdom for carrying out life's responsibilities.

Wisdom to Gain Eternal Life

God's plan of salvation is very simple. When the Philippian jailer asked Paul, "What must I do to be saved?" the apostle answered, "Believe in the Lord Jesus, and you will be saved" (Acts 16:30, 31). That's easy enough to understand!

However, the plan of salvation also involves some very profound concepts. Paul explained his understanding of salvation in the first eight chapters of Romans, and theologians have been pondering his words ever since. So how can you understand God's provision of salvation? Ask Him for wisdom. He is delighted when His children come to Him for help to understand the plan of salvation. Several concepts relative to salvation are especially important to grasp.

Justification. The first is "justification," which means that God gives us the righteousness we need in order to be acceptable to Him. As we have already pointed out, you and I can't do anything to merit God's gift of eternal life. Isaiah said that "all our righteous acts are like filthy rags" (Isa. 64:6, NIV). "The wages of sin is death" (Rom. 6:23), and no amount of good works on our part can qualify us to be acceptable to God. After pointing out that no one will be justified in God's sight by keeping the law (Rom. 3:20), Paul said, "But now a righteousness from God . . . has been made known," which "comes through faith in Jesus Christ to all who believe" (verses 21, 22, NIV). God gives you the righteousness that you need in order to meet His approval. Ellen White said that "Christ's character stands in place of your character, and you are accepted before God just as if you had not sinned."[2]

Conversion is another aspect of salvation that we need to understand. Nothing else in the Christian life will make sense to a person who has not been converted. Paul said that "the message of the cross is foolishness to those who are perishing" (1 Cor. 1:18, NIV). Why? The act of conversion changes the way people think. It transforms their minds (Rom. 12:2). That's why for converted people the message of Christ's death and resurrection is "the wisdom of God" (1 Cor. 1:24). The very same message that is foolishness to one is wisdom to the other. And the difference is the change that the Holy Spirit has wrought in the mind of the Christian, a transformation we call conversion.

In addition to a change in the way we think, conversion also gives us the power to overcome sin. That's why Paul also said that the message of the cross is "the power of God" (verse 24). Romans 1:16 assures us that "the gospel . . . is the power of God for the salvation of everyone who believes" (NIV). Most Christians are familiar with the promise in 1 Corinthians 10:13 that God "will not let you be tempted beyond what you can bear. But when you are tempted, he will also provide a way out so that you can stand up under it" (NIV). One of the most common ways God delivers us from temptation is by giving us the strength and ability to deal with it. *And this takes wisdom.* It requires a keen, godly insight to recognize our character defects and then understand how to access God's power for victory. God longs to give you that wisdom!

Sanctification. This brings us to the third aspect of salvation that God will give you wisdom to understand. Referred to as "sanctification," it concerns spiritual growth. It involves overcoming character defects so that your life comes more and more to reflect that of Jesus. God is especially eager to help you understand your flaws so that you can deal with them. And He has a special plan for doing that. It's called "conviction." Shortly before His death Jesus promised His disciples that when He returned to His Father, He would send the Holy Spirit to "convict the world of sin" (John 16:8, NKJV).

It's difficult to face our shortcomings. We may feel shame or fear because of them. Sometimes we may respond in anger when someone points them out to us. Nevertheless, there's only one way you can overcome them, and that is to acknowledge them. *And God will give you wisdom to understand them.* If you ask Him to, He will reveal your character defects to you so that you can deal with them, a process called "sanctification." God will give you wisdom to understand it.

Wisdom to Carry Out Life's Responsibilities

Life involves all kinds of responsibilities: family, work, church, community—the list goes on and on. We will consider three responsibilities for which the Bible provides wisdom and guidance.

Employees. Everybody needs to work in order to live. As soon as He created them, God gave Adam and Eve a garden to care for (Gen. 2:15). Then, after they sinned, He told them, "In the sweat of your face you shall eat bread" (Gen. 3:19, NKJV). Work has proved to be a real blessing to the human race. Solomon said, "There is nothing better for a man than to enjoy his work" (Eccl. 3:22, NIV). Paul taught that those who refuse to work have no right to eat (2 Thess. 3:10). In fact, he set an example for us by working with his own hands to support himself. That way he wouldn't be a burden to anyone (1 Thess. 2:9; 2 Thess. 3:7, 8). Jesus was about 30 years old when He entered upon His public ministry, but the people knew Him as a carpenter (Mark 6:3).

Obviously the Bible can't prescribe specific jobs for everyone. However, it lays down certain principles that can guide us in doing our work so that we will be successful. Here are several of them:

- We must do our tasks "as working for the Lord" (Col. 3:23, NIV).
- We must make good use of our time and abilities (Matt. 25:14-28).
- We must respect authority (Eph. 6:5, 6).
- We must work diligently (Prov. 12:24).

Work is both a privilege and a test for the Christian. The test is not so much in what we do as it is in *how* we do it. It is not the prestige of the job but the faithfulness with which we carry it out that counts with God.

Employers and business owners. People who own a business have unique responsibilities, and they face temptations that other people usually don't have to deal with. Businesspeople obviously want to make money or they wouldn't have established their enterprise. Some Christians view wealthy business owners with suspicion. They quote such verses as "The love of money is the root of all evil" (1 Tim. 6:10) and "It is easier for a camel to go through the eye of a needle than for a rich man to enter into the kingdom of God" (Matt. 19:24). So is it wrong to prosper in business? Absolutely not! As we hear the many appeals in our church for money, we could wish for *many* wealthy businesspeople who could respond to such requests! A number of Adventist businesspeople have donated hundreds of thousands and even millions of dollars to God's work. The Lord blessed their diligence, and they in turn glorified Him by giving.

Money is not bad in itself. It's the love of money that causes all the trouble. When we discover that we are thinking more about money than we are about our family or God, then it has begun to control us, and that will hinder our spiritual growth. The secret is to learn balance and contentment. And that's where the Bible gives wisdom. Paul said, "I have learned the secret of being content in any and every situation, whether well fed or hungry, whether living in plenty or in want" (Phil. 4:12, NIV).

According to the Bible, the Lord is the source of prosperity. Deuteronomy 8:18 says that He "gives you the ability to produce wealth" (NIV). We can truthfully say that God provides people with the *wisdom* to get wealth. While some people do inherit it and others do win thousands or even millions of dollars in the lottery, it's generally the case that wealth does not just fall into a person's lap without effort. People who succeed well in business have worked hard, and they have also worked smart. Nevertheless, we do face temptations to make money in the wrong way. Here are some examples:

- Overcharging for goods or services.
- Paying employees an unfair wage.
- Cheating on taxes.
- Manipulating business records.
- Defrauding a business partner.
- Creating shoddy, substandard products.
- Giving a short measure.

Any businessperson who follows the wisdom found in the Bible will avoid such dishonest business practices.

Summary

We have learned that the Bible provides the wisdom we need in order to live a good life. It gives us the wisdom to obtain eternal life, and it offers us the practical wisdom we must have to be good employees and good employers and business owners.

---

[1] Walter B. Knight, *Knight's Treasury of Illustrations* (Grand Rapids: Wm. B. Eerdmans, 1963), p. 425.

[2] E. G. White, *Steps to Christ,* p. 62.

CHAPTER 12

The Bible Helps Us Grow

Growth is a sign of life. Delegates to the General Conference session in St. Louis, Missouri, in 2005, understanding its importance, voted a new belief entitled "Growing in Christ." Quite a lengthy statement, it says in part, "Continually committed to Jesus as our Saviour and Lord, we are set free from the burden of our past deeds. . . . In this new freedom in Jesus, we are called to grow into the likeness of His character."

A Christian can grow through daily prayer, Bible reading, meditating, singing praises, worshipping with fellow believers, participating in mission, and giving loving service. And, indeed, every Christian *needs* to grow in Christ.

We all have no doubt heard of John Newton, the famous hymn writer who wrote "Amazing Grace." At just 19 years of age he deserted the British Navy. Later he became a slave trader on the west coast of Africa.

Struggling to survive during a severe storm at sea, Newton suddenly confronted the reality of death. From this he gained the profound insight that God, whom he had despised and denied, might exist after all. After the storm abated, he began to believe in God, even though doubts about His existence still assailed him. He struggled to believe.

Finally this swearing, ribald, blaspheming atheist surrendered to God and believed that Jesus had died for his sins. Eventually he met Alexander Clunie, who lived in London. Clunie taught Newton the Bible in a way that helped him to view it as a new book. Newton realized at last that the distant God whom he had served in fear could be a friend walking by his side. Making an unreserved surrender to Jesus, Newton became one of the best-loved hymn writers of his day. The power of the Bible transformed him from a slave trader to a hymn writer.[1]

The Need for Growth

When Nicodemus sought Jesus by night, Jesus told him that he must be

96

born again (John 3:5). At this point we would consider Nicodemus a babe in Christ. In order to progress from spiritual infancy into spiritual maturity, every newborn believer needs nurture and an opportunity to develop.

To the Ephesians Paul said, "We will no longer be infants. . . . We will in all things grow up into Him who is the Head, that is, Christ" (Eph. 4:14, 15, NIV). Peter also encouraged the early Christians to "grow in the grace and knowledge of our Lord and Savior Jesus Christ" (2 Peter 3:18, NIV).

The Bible is full of references to growth and growing. Luke describes both Jesus and John the Baptist in growth terms: "The child [John] grew, and waxed strong in spirit" (Luke 1:80) and "Jesus increased in wisdom and stature, and in favor with God and men" (Luke 2:52, NKJV). Jesus grew mentally, physically, spiritually, and socially.

Paul used growth words frequently as he urged people to enter into the full experience of life in the Spirit. He said that Christians, by "speaking the truth in love, may grow up in all things into Him who is the head—Christ" (Eph. 4:15, NKJV). Peter also appealed to the believers to "grow in the grace and knowledge of our Lord and Saviour Jesus Christ" (2 Peter 3:18). Elsewhere he urged those to whom he was writing to desire the "milk of the word" by which they would grow (1 Peter 2:2). The writer of Hebrews makes it clear that milk represents the simple, fundamental principles of the gospel (Heb. 5:12-6:1). He stressed that the believer should advance beyond elementary truths. "We are to see and understand the instruction given us by the great apostle, 'As newborn babes, desire the sincere milk of the word, that ye may grow thereby,' in perception, in likeness to the character of Christ."[2]

Second Corinthians 7:1 says that Christians are to cleanse themselves from sin, "perfecting holiness in the fear of God." The Greek word for "perfecting" means "to carry to completion or consummation," "to bring to a goal," or "to finish." Paul here speaks of growing in the present with a future goal in mind. God's Word causes us to advance and mature. "Even the most perfect Christian may increase continually in the knowledge and love of God."[3]

But "growing pains" hurt! Every Christian who grows will have painful experiences. We know that stretching or using muscles in new ways causes pain. Athletes expect sore muscles when they begin training, but strong muscles will be the result. "If those who profess the truth do not now improve their privileges and opportunities *to grow* up to the full stature of men and women in Christ Jesus, they will be no honor to the cause of truth, no honor to Christ."[4]

The Growth of Faith

Faith is one area of the Christian life in which we need to grow. What, then, is faith? Hebrew 11:1 defines it as "being sure of what we hope for and certain of what we do not see" (NIV). Faith is believing with our whole heart that God loves us, cares for us, and has our best interests in mind. It is a total trust in Him. Such faith does not mean that we believe He will give us everything we want. He may withhold things from us or even allow us to experience trials so that our "faith . . . may be proved genuine" (1 Peter 1:7, NIV).

While our wishes may not always get fulfilled, our faith in God can still grow. Consider the experience of Daniel's three friends in Babylon when pressured to worship the image of gold. Even though facing a fiery death for obeying God, they declared, "If we are thrown into the blazing furnace, the God we serve is able to save us from it, and he will rescue us from your hand, O king" (Dan. 3:17, NIV). And then they added with conviction, "But even if he does not, we want you to know, O king, that we will not serve your gods or worship the image of gold you have set up" (verse 18, NIV). Although they believed that God had the *ability* to rescue them, they still left the decision in His hands, trusting that whatever happened would be for their ultimate good and His glory. A growing faith shows maturity to accept any situation with full trust in God, no matter what happens.

God is the source of faith, but humans must decide to put their trust in Him. Faith develops through the study of God's Word (Rom. 10:17), but we must take the time and put forth the effort to study it. The more we explore the Word of God, the more we know God. The more we know Him, the more we will love Him. The more we love Him, the more we will trust Him. And the more we trust Him, the easier it will be to do whatever He wants us to do.

Growing in Love

Scripture says that we are to love God with all our heart, soul, and mind (Matt. 22:37), and our neighbors as ourselves (verse 39). It commands us to love our fellow believers (John 13:35), and it even challenges us to love our enemies (Matt. 5:44)! It is not easy to follow such stipulations, because we've been born with a selfish nature. Paul said that in the last days people would be "lovers of their own selves" (2 Tim. 3:2). Normally we love those who love us, but a unique scriptural teaching says that we are no different than the heathen if we love only those who love us (Matt. 5:47). We should grow in our experience until we can love the unlovable. "As your love for Him increases, your love for each other will grow deeper and stronger."[5]

Also we must mature in our understanding and experience of "love." We use the word so often that it is easy to lose sight of what it actually means. Biblical examples reveal that love is something we *do* rather than an emotion or something we *feel*. First Corinthians 13 shows some of the attitudes and actions of love. True godly love:

> Is kind.
> Doesn't boast.
> Isn't proud.
> Isn't rude.
> Keeps no record of wrongs.
> Rejoices in the truth.
> Always trusts.
> Always hopes.
> Never fails.

The Bible gives an example of redemptive love: "This is how we know what love is: Jesus laid down his life for us" (1 John 3:16, NIV). When we love at this level, we will forget all about our own rights, interests, and hurts. We will be willing, as Jesus was, to sacrifice everything for the sake of the one we love, and we will even be able to love our enemies (Matt. 5:44-48). In spite of the painful things people have done to us, we still can care for them and seek to promote their well-being.

The Bible records Jesus' command to "love your neighbor" (Matt. 22:39). Our neighbor is not necessarily likable, related to us, or somebody that we would have chosen as a friend. In the parable of the good Samaritan (Luke 10:29-37) Jesus taught that our neighbor is the next individual we meet who is in need. That person may be someone who hates us, or it may be a total stranger, but God commands us to love him or her. In Romans 12:20 Paul said, " 'If your enemy is hungry, feed him; if he is thirsty, give him something to drink. In doing this, you will heap burning coals on his head.' Do not be overcome by evil, but overcome evil with good" (verse 21, NIV).

Recall the hardest people to love that you ever met, or try to remember ones who deliberately wronged you in the past—maybe individuals who for their own selfish motives hurt you. How can you overcome your resentment and honestly love them with redemptive love? Begin by praying for them. As you grow, you might help them if an opportunity arises. Do you think that remembering the experience of Jesus during His last day on earth would help you to react positively to your enemies and wish the best for them? Jesus died for them as well as for you and me. In Him we all have the same value.

Growing in Christ

Children in Sabbath school sing, "Jesus loves me! this I know." The Bible tells us of Jesus, the Creator and King of the universe, who loves us and died for us. "For God so loved the world that he gave his one and only Son, that whoever believes in him shall not perish but have eternal life" (John 3:16, NIV). Have we forgotten the excitement of this important text? How can we maintain the thrill of reading it? By growing in Christ!

Such growth in Christ means more than just knowing Him. It includes being (acting) like Him in our words, deeds, and even our thoughts. Paul wrote to the Romans that we are called to be like Christ (Rom. 8:29).

"Our growth in grace, our joy, our usefulness—all depend upon our union with Christ. It is by communion with Him, daily, hourly—by abiding in Him—that we are to grow in grace."[6]

One characteristic of growing in Christ is surrendering ourselves to Him. "I have been crucified with Christ and I no longer live, but Christ lives in me. The life I live in the body, I live by faith in the Son of God, who loved me and gave himself for me" (Gal. 2:20, NIV). According to Paul here, there is a sense in which we do not live—that is, we no longer control our own lives. Our decisions are no longer based only on what we think. Christ is now Lord of our lives. This growing experience needs to be ours until we have finally developed a Christlike character.

We can grow in Christ by reading the Scriptures, especially the Gospels. As we do so, we may ask the following questions: (1) What is Jesus is saying here? (2) What did this mean to those who heard Him in the first century? (3) What does it mean to us in the twenty-first century? (4) What does it mean to me personally? By spending more time with the Word of God, we will have an expanding experience in our spiritual life and in our relationship with Christ.

Ellen White said, "By faith you are to grow up in Him—by giving and taking. You are to *give* all—your heart, your will, your service, give yourself to Him to obey all His requirements; and you must *take* all—Christ, the fullness of all blessing, to abide in your heart, to be your strength, your righteousness, your everlasting helper, to give you power to obey."[7]

Growing in the Spirit

Earlier in this chapter we observed that a Christian's life begins with the new birth (John 3:3). When Nicodemus asked, "How can a man be born when he is old?" Jesus replied that "no one can enter the kingdom of God unless he is born of water and the Spirit" (verse 5, NIV). Born of water represents baptism and born of the Spirit is conversion, which means that the Holy Spirit infills us at the moment of spiritual birth. As a baby needs to grow, the newly baptized member must develop in the Spirit. The task of the Holy Spirit in our lives is to "guide . . . into all truth" (John 16:13). One way the Spirit does so is by reminding us of the things that the Bible teaches, because the Word of God is truth (John 17:17). The Spirit also leads us to recognize our own condition. "When he [the Holy Spirit] comes, he will convict the world of guilt in regard to sin and righteousness and judgment" (John 16:8, NIV). The Spirit brings our sin to our awareness through our study of the Scriptures. One of the functions of the law of God is to reveal sin. "If it had not been for the law, I should not have known sin" (Rom. 7:7, RSV).

As we grow in Christian living, we will also mature in the Spirit. We will become more sensitive to sin and to the voice of God in our hearts. The Bible gives a few of the important steps that must happen for the Spirit to take charge of our lives. They include:

- *Having a desire to be filled with the Spirit.* "Blessed are those who hunger and thirst for righteousness, for they will be filled" (Matt. 5:6, NIV).
- *Not allowing unconfessed sin to remain in your life.* First John 1:9 tells us that "if we confess our sins, he is faithful and just and will forgive us our sins and purify us from all unrighteousness" (NIV). One of the Holy Spirit's roles is convincing us of the reality of our sins. Unpardonable sin is unconfessed sin, which becomes the sin against the Holy Spirit.
- *Asking the Holy Spirit to fill you.* Remember the experience of the apostles at Pentecost? Not until they prayed for the Holy Spirit did He fill them (Acts 1:14; 2:1-4).
- *Living according to the voice of the Spirit.* The Bible says, "Live by the Spirit, and you will not gratify the desires of the sinful nature" (Gal. 5:16, NIV).
- *Thanking God for filling you with the Holy Spirit* (1 Cor. 15:57).

Summary

The Bible is the source of our spiritual development. The more time we spend with the Word of God, the more we will grow in our faith and love. As we grow in the Spirit we will be more sensitive and responsive to His voice in our lives. Through His power we will also experience growth in faith and love, becoming more like Jesus until we reach the maturity He wants us to achieve.

---

[1] John Pollock, "From Slave Trader to Hymn Writer," in *Practical Christianity,* ed. LaVonne Neff et al., pp. 75-78.

[2] Ellen G. White, *Medical Ministry* (Mountain View, Calif.: Pacific Press Pub. Assn., 1932), p. 124.

[3] White, *Testimonies,* vol. 1, p. 340.

[4] *Ibid.,* vol. 4, p. 359. (Italics supplied.)

[5] Ellen G. White, *The Adventist Home* (Washington, D.C.: Review and Herald Pub. Assn., 1952), p. 106.

[6] White, *Steps to Christ,* p. 69.

[7] *Ibid.,* p. 70.

CHAPTER 13

The Bible Exists Forever

Vladimir the Great was baptized by immersion in the Dnieper River in Kiev in A.D. 988, and he introduced Christianity to his country, Russia. Consequently Russia was historically considered a "spiritual" nation. However, the situation changed when the Bolshevik revolution occurred in October 1917. The *Communist Manifesto* became the people's "Bible," the leaders of the Communist Party were their saints, and Lenin was their savior. The real Bible was forbidden, and the notorious KGB imprisoned, tortured, and sent Christians to concentration camps. "Cautious historians estimate the death toll in the camps at 10-20 million (Solzhenitsyn put the figure at roughly 60-70 million). In Stalin's era, over 40,000 priests are said to have lost their lives. Ninety-eight of every 100 Orthodox churches were closed."[1]

Roland Hegstad has reported that "of the 3,000 Seventh-day Adventists sent to prison camps, only about 500 returned. Of 179 pastors sent into exile in 1929, only four returned. One old church member from Kiev, Galena, described the tragic situation this way: 'One Sabbath, the police came during the church service. They took every grandfather, every father, every husband, every male over 18. We never saw them again. We were like a church without men. Wives without husbands. Children without fathers. Sisters without brothers. Through the years ours became a church of old women. Old women . . . who never forgot their faith in God or their hope of reunion someday.'"[2] In spite of persecution, many Christians remained committed to Christ, affirmed their faith in God, and, to save their Bibles, hid them. However, the Word of God couldn't remain hidden! In August 1991 Russia's spiritual revolution began. The Bible is correct when it says, "The word of the Lord stands forever" (1 Peter 1:25, NIV).

The Bible Cannot Be Destroyed

David wrote, "Long ago I learned from your statutes that you established them to last forever" (Ps. 119:152, NIV). Yes, God did intend His law to endure forever. The Bible has faced many challenges from the beginning of its existence until the present time. What happened in Russia was only one of the many such instances. Throughout history people have tried to destroy the Bible, but all such efforts have failed.

In A.D. 303 the Roman emperor Diocletian issued an edict to stop Christians from worshipping and to call for the burning of their Scriptures. During the French Revolution, Voltaire predicted that in less than 100 years Christianity would be swept from existence and pass into history.[3] He also said that the Bible was an exploded book. In reality we find that it is his theory that has exploded, for he died more than 200 years ago, but the Bible is still here.

Robert Ingersoll, a man of great talent, declared that the Bible would not be read in 10 years, but he died long ago, and the Bible today is still the world's best seller. The philosopher David Hume thought that Christianity would be dead in 20 years. A meeting of the Bible Society in Edinburgh convened in the very room where he took his last breath! Thomas Paine, the noted agnostic, predicted that in five years no one would be able to find a Bible in the United States.[4] Today millions of homes and most hotel and motel rooms have Bibles.

When Jeremiah received God's revelation about the destruction of Judah, he dictated the message to Baruch, who wrote it on a scroll. That warning was read in front of Jehoiakim, king of Judah. In response, the ruler cut the scroll in pieces with a knife and cast it into the fire, where it burned to ashes (Jer. 36)—but its predictions all came true!

The fascinating story of Christianity's growth in Madagascar could fill many pages. A brief summary will give you a glimpse into history. Roman Catholics first introduced missionaries to that country in the sixteenth century. Portuguese Jesuits and French Lazarists followed in the seventeenth and eighteenth centuries. The London Missionary Society sent its first missionaries, Pastor David Jones and Thomas Bevan, in 1818. Enjoying the protection of King Radama I (1810-1828), they opened a school that succeeded in attracting many young people from noble Malagasy families. In subsequent years many more schools opened. One of their important achievements was reducing the Malagasy language to Latin script, then publishing the Bible.

Mission work continued until the reign of Queen Ranavalona I, under whom brutal persecution began. In 1835, the same year as the publication of the Malagasy Bible, the missionaries found themselves forced to leave the country, and many Malagasy converts suffered martyrdom. Christians could not have Bibles in their homes.

Did persecution rid the country of Bibles? Have Bibles disappeared in Madagascar? As predicted, the Bible shall exist forever. Both Ranavalona I's son and Queen Ranavalona II favored Christianity, and large numbers of the upper class followed Queen Ranavalona II's example in converting to Christianity. The number of Christians grew from 5,000 in 1861 to 1 million in 1900. Today nearly half of Madagascar's 18 million people are Christians, and one can find the Bible in all parts of Madagascar. *The Bible definitely cannot be destroyed.*

The Bible Is Applicable Today

The Bible says that "everything that was written in the past was written to teach us, so through endurance and the encouragement of the Scriptures we might have hope" (Rom. 15:4, NIV). However, many people have said quite bluntly that they do not believe that the Bible is applicable today, that it has no relevance at all in modern times. They claim, for example:

- that the Old Testament is about 3,000 years old and the New Testament is about 1,900 years old. How can teachings that ancient have any relevance in the twenty-first century?
- that the Bible came from Palestine, a narrow territory that stretched only 150 miles from north to south and 65 miles from east to west. The teaching from such a small territory cannot speak to people all over the world.
- that Bible times were extremely different from the present-day world. Living conditions and the mobility and activities of the people have radically changed.

However, even with differences of time, geography, situation, and living conditions, people who trust the Word of God will accept its validity. In his book *Ethics in a Permissive Society* the late William Barclay mentioned three ways that the Bible is still relevant today:

- The external environment can alter while the underlying principles remain the same. Take, for example, buildings. There are a lot of differences between the Parthenon in Athens, the Canterbury Cathedral in London, and the pyramids in Egypt. Externally they are dissimilar. However, the principles of structure in each building follow the same laws of architecture. Otherwise, they would simply collapse. The externals can be very different, but the underlying principle is the same.

- The Bible teaches Christian ethics regarding personal relationships between men and men, men and women, women and women, and men and women and God. The aspects of human relationships do not change through time. They consist of love and hate, honor and shame, loyalty and betrayal. Such characteristics have remained the same from Bible times to the present. For example, when Rebekah arrived to marry Isaac, she rode on a camel, wore Eastern robes, and covered her face. Today's bride shows up at the wedding in a rented limousine wearing a dress. However, the situation is exactly the same: two young people in love who dedicate themselves to each other for life. The Bible's principles of relationships will not alter as long as men are men, women are women, and God is God.
- The Bible teaches Christian ethics in community. It is almost impossible for a person to live in isolation from other people. Love, loyalty, forgiveness, and service are community matters that must always be practiced when people live together. Whenever these principles are ignored, the community breaks down and eventually ceases to exist. This principle does not change, whether people have different levels of education, different colors of skin, or different cultural backgrounds.[5]

God's Everlasting Plan

God never changes, and He has an eternal plan for every one of His created beings. His immutable plans extend from the beginning to the end of time. Consider the following verses:

Proverbs 19:21—It is the Lord's purpose that prevails.
Isaiah 46:11—God has planned long ago.
Isaiah 46:11—What He has decided to do, that He will bring to pass.
Acts 5:39—If it is from God, who will be able to stop it?
Hebrews 6:17—God wanted to make the unchanging nature of His purpose very clear.
Psalm 102:27—God always remains the same.
Hebrews 13:8—Jesus remains the same yesterday, today, and forever.
Hebrews 1:12—He remains the same, and His years will never end.
Psalm 33:11—The plans of the Lord stand firm forever.

As our Creator, God, who is omnipotent, omniscient, and infinite, loves us with an everlasting love (Jer. 31:3). His eternal plan includes salvation for everyone. In a somewhat difficult passage, Paul tells us in Ephesians 1:4-14: "He chose us in him before the creation of the world to be holy and blameless in his sight. In love he predestined us to be adopted as his sons through Jesus Christ. . . . And you also were included in Christ when you heard the word of truth, the gospel of your salvation. Having believed, you were marked in him with a seal, the promised Holy Spirit, who is a deposit guaranteeing our inheritance until the redemption" (NIV). God has predestined every one of us to be His sons and daughters by adoption, predestined us to be holy and blameless. "God is love" (1 John 4:8), and He planned for each of us to live with Him forever (1 John 2:25).

Unbroken Promises

How thankful we can be that God's promises remain unbroken! The Bible has thousands of promises from Genesis to Revelation. Unlike humans, who often break their word, God always keeps His. King Solomon, in his prayer, said, "Praise be to the Lord, who has given rest to his people Israel just as He has promised. Not one word has failed" (1 Kings 8:56, NIV). Paul echoed the same thought, telling us that he was "fully persuaded that God had power to do what he had promised" (Rom. 4:21, NIV). God will work out His promises in His own time.

The Lord has vowed to meet our every need, whether in good times or in crisis. Notice the Bible's promises for these various situations:

John 16:33—when you are in trouble.
Lamentations 3:19-24—when the future seems hopeless.
Proverbs 3:5, 6—when your faith needs strengthening.
Matthew 7:7—when you need answers to prayers.
Matthew 28:20—when you need a sense of His presence.
Mark 9:23—when you are seeking unlimited blessings.
Luke 17:6—when you need obstacles removed.
John 6:35—when you desire spiritual fullness.
Romans 1:16—when you long for salvation.
Hebrew 2:18—when you need help for overcoming temptation.

They are just a sampling of the promises you will find in the Bible, all of which apply to all of us today and are relevant to our lives even in our modern society.

Although we face many problems, God's promises provide encouragement and comfort and give us power to help us overcome life's obstacles. "It is in these promises that Christ communicates to us His grace and power. They are leaves from the tree which is 'for the healing of the nations.' Rev. 22:2. Received, assimilated, they are to be the strength of the character, the inspiration and sustenance of the life. Nothing else can have such healing power."[6]

The Bible and Persecution

Those who uphold their Bible and faith in Christ have faced persecution ever since Christianity began. Jesus predicted, "You will be handed over to the courts. You will be flogged in synagogues. You will be summoned to appear before governors and kings on my account. . . . Do not worry. . . . Brother will betray brother to death, and the father his child; children will turn against their parents and send them to their death. All will hate you for your allegiance to me; but the man who holds out to the end will be saved" (Mark 13:9-13, NEB).

The words of Jesus came true almost immediately. Shortly after Pentecost, Peter and John encountered trouble in the Temple and found themselves thrown into prison. Then Stephen was stoned to death (Acts 7:54-60). At Lystra Paul was stoned so severely that the onlookers thought he was dead (Acts 14:19), and the Romans finally executed him for preaching the Word. Peter would have died for his faith had an angel not delivered him from prison the night before his execution (Acts 12:3-19). The 10 years of the Diocletian persecution (A.D. 303-313) nearly annihilated the church. During the Middle Ages thousands of Christians perished because of their love and devotion to the Bible. Even the possession of a copy of the Bible was sufficient to condemn a person to torture and death by burning at the stake.

Both before and during the time of reformation John Wycliffe, John Huss, Ulrich Zwingli, and other Reformers endured persecution for preaching God's truth, and some were martyred. They went to their death with amazing courage, always thinking of others rather than themselves. William Tyndale translated the Bible. The bishop of London ordered the destruction of all copies of Tyndale's translation. Later Tyndale himself was strangled and burned at the stake.[7]

The United Bible Societies reports that "at the start of the nineteenth century, Scriptures were available in just 68 languages. Today, Scriptures are available in no less than 2,403 languages; with the complete Bible having been translated into at least 426 languages, and the New Testament into some 1,115. In addition, parts of the Bible . . . have been made available in 862 languages."[8] The annual circulation of the Bible is approximately 4.5 million copies. It is clear that Scripture is correct when it states that "the grass withers and the flowers fall, but the word of our God stands forever" (Isa. 40:8, NIV).

Summary

Truly we can believe that the Bible is fully inspired and has authority to reveal the eternal will of God. As our "owner's manual," it has practical guidelines for our lives, helping us to be happy. Because the Bible is the Word of God, it will endure forever, even as God exists forever. But unless we again become "people of the Book," of what value is the Bible to us? In this book we have explored internal evidence of the Bible's inspiration. We have looked at the external evidences that archaeology and science provide. And we have seen that God's prophecies and promises are sure. Let us resolve to spend time each day with the Word, so that we may personally benefit from all that the Bible has to offer!

[1] Mark Finley, *The Cross and the Kremlin* (Fallbrook, Calif.: Hart Research Center, 1992), p. 18.
[2] *Ibid.*
[3] http://www.truthmagazine.com/archives/volume18/TM018262.htm.
[4] http://www.nothernwatchdog.com/WDogYouthArticle5.htm.
[5] See William Barclay, *Ethics in a Permissive Society* (London: Collins, 1971), pp. 29, 30.
[6] E. G. White, *The Ministry of Healing,* p. 122.
[7] Arthur S. Maxwell, *Courage for the Crisis* (Mountain View, Calif.: Pacific Press Pub. Assn., 1962), pp. 137-140; see also http://en.wikipedia.org/wiki/William_Tyndale.
[8] http://www.biblesociety.org/trans-gr.htm.

CLEAR WORD

OTHER PRODUCTS YOU MIGHT ENJOY

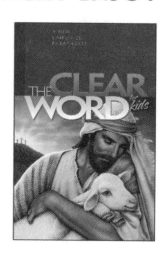